What a MAN Wants, What a Woman Needs

The Secret to Successful, Fulfilling Relationships

Eddie Long

THOMAS NELSON PUBLISHERS®
Nashville

A Division of Thomas Nelson, Inc.
www.ThomasNelson.com

I dedicate this book to my Lord and Savior, Jesus Christ.

Also, I dedicate this to my wife, Vanessa Long, my sons Eric, Edward and Jared, and my daughter Taylor—Thank you for unselfishly allowing me to give myself to the world. I also give a special thanks to the New Birth Missionary Baptist Church congregation in Lithonia, Georgia.

———————

Published in Nashville, Tennessee, by Thomas Nelson, Inc., P.O. Box 141000, Nashville, Tennessee 37214.

Unless otherwise noted, Scripture quotations are from THE NEW KING JAMES VERSION. Copyright © 1979, 1980, 1982, Thomas Nelson, Inc., Publishers.

Library on Congress Cataloging-in-Publication Data

Long, Eddie.
    What a man wants, what a woman needs : the secret to successful, fulfilling relationships / Eddie Long.
       p. cm.
    Includes bibliographical references.
    ISBN 0-7852-6572-4
    1. Marriage—Biblical teaching. 2. Man—woman relationships—Biblical teaching. I. Title.
BX680.M35 L66 2002
248.4—dc21   2002003334

Printed in the United States of America
03 04 05 06 PHX 6 5

CONTENTS

Foreword   iv

chapter 1 · What a Man Wants   1

chapter 2 · What Do You Believe?   22

chapter 3 · What a Woman Needs   40

chapter 4 · The Missing Element of the Kingdom   57

chapter 5 · Men, We're Hiding   76

chapter 6 · Women: Life Givers and Walking Epistles   101

chapter 7 · Dating the Devil   117

chapter 8 · How Many People Are in Your Bed?   137

chapter 9 · To Know   150

chapter 10 · Pulled Aside for a Date with Destiny   168

chapter 11 · Passion for Life   187

chapter 12 · Kingdom Men, Kingdom Women   206

Notes   215

About the Author   218

FOREWORD

M arriage can be the closest thing to heaven or hell on this earth."

Such honest observations and statements make Bishop Long's book *What a Man Wants, What a Woman Needs* a must-read.

No platitudes here. No easy formula-driven solutions—only a biblically based call to kingdom living.

Bishop Long's thesis—the missing element in the kingdom of God is real kingdom men and real kingdom women—relates to every Christian home.

Calling men to be responsible is a timely message when many men have stepped down from their godly servant leadership roles in their homes. Calling women to become "walking epistles" is a message of hope for our world's future.

Fidelity, purity, servanthood, responsibility, covenant keeping, and rising beyond your failures are just some of the challenges issued by Bishop Long.

Most important, Bishop Long calls on the kingdom, an army of prayer warriors, prophets, preachers, evangelists, pastors, and teachers anointed to work together, with no place for ego.

Bishop Long's honesty and vulnerability make this book authentic and powerful.

It is my joy to call Eddie L. Long my brother and friend. And it is my privilege to recommend his life-changing message to you.

Dr. John C. Maxwell
Author, Speaker and Founder
The INJOY Group

Chapter 1

WHAT A MAN WANTS

S ome things are just naturally interesting. As much as half of the world's population at any given time in human history have thought about "what a man wants."[1] The response that immediately comes to mind—that a man wants sex—is only a part of the answer.

We could probably find a hundred different versions of this chapter title adorning the covers of the world's magazines and tabloids every month—along with ten times as many "pop" answers to the quiz. However, I wonder how many of the writers, researchers, and editors would turn to the ultimate Source for the right answer.

I'm convinced that most men long for something they would find nearly impossible to describe on their own. The truth is that we all need help defining our chief longings. We can assemble a certain amount of information on our own, but we need to go to the Original Equipment Manufacturer's Manual to help us finish the job.

Men don't ask for much (just ask one). With virtually no regard to his own appearance, manners, or attractiveness, every man secretly hopes for a woman whose beauty takes his breath away and jump-starts his heart at first sight.

Of course, he also hopes she possesses a liberal dose of his mother's ways to care for the little boy lingering inside his hulking shell (and hidden far from view). Naturally, he also expects his ideal woman to be the world's best lover, the best cook in town, his lifetime best friend, and his most loyal supporter all rolled into one neat package.

That's not asking for much, is it? The answer is yes and no. First, we must accept the inevitable reality check: Sir, no woman on earth has what it takes to totally fulfill you.

God gives men and women just enough of Himself, just enough mystery, spice, or something nice, to make us take notice of one another. Yet at most, each of us possesses just a few pieces of the puzzle, and they will never be enough to satisfy. Why? God expects us to "come home" every day and linger in His presence.

The core of every true desire and longing (before they get perverted or tainted by evil or magnified by our own foolish choices) is our deep hunger for our Creator. David the prophet, priest, and king said, "As the deer pants for the water brooks, so pants my soul for You, O God" (Ps. 42:1).

A KINGDOM MAN LOOKS FOR FAR MORE

Second, what a man wants varies directly with the nature of the man doing the wanting. A kingdom man, whose mind, will, and appetites have been honed and realigned by the Word of God, will look for *far more* in a potential wife than will a man of the flesh and the unsaved world.

Our culture leaves very little for the imagination to work on when it comes to what a worldly man wants. Basically, it boils down to sex and control. If it sounds animalistic, that's because it is.

Yet even an animalistic, worldly man can't help responding when he comes across a kingdom member of the *other half* who lives and walks according to God's plan. As far as I can tell, everyone sits up and takes notice when a kingdom woman walks into a room. There is something about a godly woman that makes you want to put a capital *W* in front of the word *Woman*.

Now, I don't want anyone to think a kingdom man is hormonally dead. If a man is living as he should in the sight of God, his hormonal balance is better than most. He just refuses to let hormones drive his car. He has a much longer and more important want list than the single-page cheat sheet most men carry—the one titled "Sexual Attraction."

He Wants a Kingdom Woman

Perhaps we should rephrase the question driving this chapter to read: What does a kingdom man want? That automatically provides the answer: He wants a kingdom woman.

If you want to know what a kingdom woman is, you have to talk with the King. Fortunately, He has a lot to say about the women in His kingdom. In fact, He put it right up front where all the action began.

You don't have to be a Bible scholar or college graduate to gather from the book of Genesis that when God made man, He went to the dirt (Gen. 2:7). Adam's sons are still a little dusty and funky—especially when they've been working in the noonday sun or doing physical labor. The modern models come in all colors, sizes, and shapes, but all of them still have Adam's earthy ability to be downright nasty to those with more refined tastes and fresher deodorant.

Now God didn't use dirt to make the first woman. He had a *better idea.* As soon as He got Adam fully equipped, He said, "Adam, lie down."

Adam said, "What? I ain't tired."

God said, "Go to sleep, Adam. Go to sleep, son. I've got something for you after you wake up. Boy, do I have something for you! Go to sleep, son. Christmastime is coming."

Then Adam underwent a serious operation:

> The LORD God caused a deep sleep to fall on Adam, and he slept; and He took one of his ribs, and closed up the flesh in its place. *Then the rib which the LORD God had taken from man He made into a woman, and He brought her to the man.* And Adam said:
>
> "This is now bone of my bones
> And flesh of my flesh;
> She shall be called Woman,
> Because she was taken out of Man."
>
> Therefore a man shall leave his father and mother and be joined to his wife, and they shall become one flesh. And

they were both naked, the man and his wife, and were not ashamed. (Gen. 2:21–25, emphasis mine)

God made Adam first and gave him specific instructions about the proper order of things in His Garden. Once Adam was full of God's instructions and personal impartation, and when Eve was full of God and able to walk as a helpmate or custom-designed companion for Adam, He put them together.

BONE! FLESH! THAT'S MINE!

They knew the score instantly. They didn't need any manuals, videos, or seminars. They just knew. Adam saw Eve and said, "Bone! Flesh! That's *mine!* That's part of me." He *knew* it. He didn't have to *date* to find that out. He just *knew.* When Adam saw Eve, he said, "Whoa, man. Oh, God, now *this* is *good.* It's a good thing. This is better than the trees and the bumblebees and the buffarillas. Whoa! This is a what, Lord? You want me to name it? Okay, God. Now, she is the only one in the Garden that makes me stop in my tracks and causes my heart to skip a beat, so I'm calling this one a Whoa-Man!"

Now Eve hadn't been to the beauty shop yet, and she hadn't even had her nails done. She hadn't had a pedicure since creation, and she hadn't been to Bally's Health Spa yet either. Come to think of it, she hadn't made a single trip to Saks Fifth Avenue. She didn't need a wardrobe because Eve was just *fine* in her "Eveness." If you could ask Adam, he would say she was *real fine.*

What do we see in Adam's custom-crafted companion that

seems to be missing from most of the women in our day? Is God trying to tell us that women are investing more time primping, parading, and masquerading to fix the outside when the real worth and value on the inside are missing or messed up? (Yes, He is saying the same thing to many men today.)

Pretty (but Empty) Wrappers Attract Random Samplers

Ladies, if your "inside woman" is messed up or missing in action, then that outside wrapper won't attract *much* worth keeping (in terms of men). Your pretty wrapper might attract a shopper or a random sampler or two for a while, but sooner or later they'll discover there isn't anything in the box!

Thousands of years after God introduced Adam to the ideal woman, Peter shared his "kingdom-woman shopping list" with us. It helps kingdom men know what to look for, and it also helps kingdom women discover who and what they are—if they have the courage to receive it. This is really a shopping list of godly traits found only in kingdom women:

> Wives, likewise, be submissive to your own husbands, that even if some do not obey the word, they, without a word, may be won by the conduct of their wives, when they observe your chaste conduct accompanied by fear. *Do not let your adornment be merely outward*—arranging the hair, wearing gold, or putting on fine apparel—rather let it be *the hidden person of the heart,* with the *incorruptible*

beauty of a gentle and quiet spirit, which is *very precious* in the sight of God. For in this manner, in former times, the holy women who trusted in God also adorned themselves, being submissive to their own husbands, as Sarah obeyed Abraham, calling him lord, whose daughters you are if you do good and are not afraid with any terror. (1 Peter 3:1–6, emphasis mine)

DON'T DISMISS YOUR RESISTANCE TO GOD'S WORD

Let me stop the parade to ask you a question: When you read the passage from Peter's epistle, did you feel a curious resistance pass through your mind? If you did, don't dismiss your resistance to God's Word as unimportant.

Remember that you weren't reading Eddie Long's opinions about men and woman; you were reading an apostolic letter in God's Word. The things in this epistle are echoed throughout the Bible. Logically, that means that the Bible is wrong, or that you are unconsciously resisting something that is *godly* and *right.* Just keep that in mind as we continue.

What did Peter mean when he said "adorning"? Is all makeup taboo for kingdom women? No. Peter used a Greek word, *kosmeo,* which literally means "to put in proper order, to decorate, to adorn, garnish, or trim."[2] He was saying, "Don't put all of your focus on your cosmetics or the way you arrange your stuff and place things on your body."

We often have women who receive Christ and enter our church services in greater Atlanta as new Christians who are dressed as if they are still on the "outside." They were saved that weekend outside the club and started coming to church.

You have to give these new sisters in Christ a little leeway. They don't know any better, so they walk into church services wearing their best "catch a man's eye and make him sigh" outfits. If you look down another row, you'll see women who *do know better* wearing something just as low up top and high down below.

IF HE IS HUMAN, THEN HE IS FUMIN'

I pity the kingdom man sitting anywhere close by. Just ask yourself a question: Is that righteous man more focused on the message or on who is sitting next to him? If he is *human,* then he is fumin'. He is definitely having a struggle.

God gave Eve and every woman after her such power and beauty in their natural state that "stuff starts happening" whenever they get together with men. God is saying, "Please understand that you are *human.* I created you complete with hormones and the ability to function at the junction with all of the unction." We have enough temptation as it is. There is no need to add more enticement to what is already *good.*

Why did I bring this up? Women in the church are often indistinguishable from women in the world. They strut their stuff with all of the overt sexuality you would find in any club, singles bar, or sensual movie scene. They assume that kingdom men are looking for the same thing worldly men look for. Seeing these women, kingdom men sometimes have a tough time keeping their minds on the King and the kingdom.

Can I be real with you? I'm a preacher, and I serve as a bishop in my fellowship of churches. Yet even the bishop has to work extra hard at avoiding evil when I try to preach to a congregation spiked with Eves all dressed to kill. If I try to look into the eyes of folks on a pew, sometimes I have to keep my eyes staring at the lights or the seams of the carpet—I have to look like an idiot just to keep my eyes *out of the trouble* hanging out in the pew.

Jerked Out of the Spirit by "a Sight That Ain't Right"

I was Eddie Long first, long before any other titles came along. Sometimes I walk down the aisles preaching, and I'm suddenly jerked out of the Spirit by "a sight that ain't right," something I just don't need to see! I literally have to run back to the altar, saying, "Lord, have mercy!"

Kingdom men are looking for kingdom women. Yet women in the kingdom still talk like women in the world: "How do I look, girlfriend?"

Then girlfriend says, "You look sexy."

That brings a smile and the satisfied reply, "Oh, good."

As humans, we want to feel sexy, but some of us take it too far. Whew! Where are those funeral-home fans when you need them? Paul said something we all need to hear regularly: "Flee sexual immorality" (1 Cor. 6:18). Unfortunately, people don't seem to understand what Paul was saying.

In our day, men don't seem to chase women anymore; women run after them. I don't understand it. I look at them, and I want to say, "Girl, you are too pretty to be chasing *him*. What do you want *that* thing for?"

We have a whole generation of women who don't know how to define who they are other than by how they dress. Their identities are locked into their appearances, and that is a prescription for disaster. It seems that half the women in America are depressed because they don't match the MTV video profiles or the latest looks on MTV or BET. Their world is coming to an end because they can't copy what they see on any of the countless music videos flooding the airways featuring half-naked women and want-to-be-naked men bouncing to a sensual beat.

NOTHING FINER THAN A KINGDOM WOMAN IN THE KNOW

If you want to *become* what real kingdom men are looking for, ladies, listen to what God is saying: "Spend time finding out who you are." There is nothing *finer* than a kingdom woman who *knows* who she is.

A kingdom man is looking for a *real woman* who knows who she is. He is looking for a woman with high standards, a woman who will not accept trash. A woman who knows who she is will say:

"You don't call me at eleven-thirty at night. If you can't call me at a decent time, then don't bother to call me. Don't lie to me and don't be late. If anything, come early because I am *precious*. No, don't even think about touching this. *This* is not to be touched. *This* is costly. The character in this body is so costly that it cannot be contaminated. I spent time with God, and I know why He called me. If you aren't called, too, then don't call at all."

A Quiet Spirit: The Secret to a Kingdom Woman's Power

Why are kingdom women so hard to find today? We've mixed the values of an unholy culture with the unmixed values of a holy King. It is like trying to mix oil with water. It doesn't work. Peter said a quiet spirit is the secret to a kingdom woman's power. The world sees things differently (and wrongly).

Most thoroughly modern women today are studying to be *smart*, not *wise*. Knowledge is good until it comes into conflict with godly wisdom. Smart women become unwise women when they acquire knowledge for the sole purpose of competing with men.

I'm not telling women to bypass an education or to work only inside the home. I'm saying what the Bible says: "Wisdom is the principal thing; therefore get wisdom. And in all your getting, get understanding" (Prov. 4:7).

What does a man want? He wants a kingdom woman, a companion of the heart *custom created* to help him establish God's kingdom on earth as it is in heaven. What do most men get? They get worldly women equipped and encouraged by the culture to compete, argue, nag, and battle *against them* for supremacy in every area. Last time I checked, the Bible still said, "Every kingdom divided against itself is brought to desolation, and every city or house divided against itself will not stand" (Matt. 12:25).

God told Eve after the Fall, "Your desire shall be for your

husband, and he shall rule over you" (Gen. 3:16). Regardless of what women do or how much the feminist movement demonstrates and infiltrates the culture, wives and women in general can never rule men. Yes, they will successfully run their men out of their houses and lives. Their men may sleep on the roof or leave the house for good, but those women will never rule their men.

It is in a man's original nature to rule, give battle, dominate, and conquer. These are the tools God gave men to conquer and dominate the earth.

THE PERFECT GOD-GIVEN TOOL TO DISARM MASCULINE WEAPONRY

"Why do I have such a hard time dealing with my husband or other men?"

It's because a man is a warrior. When another man hits me or starts to compete with me, the testosterone begins to flow, and the battle is on. God gave kingdom women the perfect tool to totally disarm all of this masculine weaponry—if they will use it.

How does a woman deal with a man? Quietly. My wife knows exactly how to deal with me on those odd days when I seem determined to have an argument. (Bishop or not, I still have those days. Spell that illness *h-u-m-a-n.*)

When there's no one else around to argue with but my wife, I'll start arguing, but she won't argue back. She lets me go on until I finally come to my senses and look at her to ask, "Look, what's up?"

Then she will say, "I would have to stoop very low to get on your level." Then she goes about her business. That shuts me up every time. I don't know how to respond to that because it wasn't a fight. It was a quiet word from a *woman of wisdom.*

Basically, she communicated to me a volume of things: "If you want to talk, bring it down. If you want to reason together, I'm open. If you want to be mature, I'll talk to you. Until you make up your mind on those things, I'm going on about my business."

The power of a kingdom woman is not in her volume, knowledge, or exceptional powers of argumentation. She almost certainly possesses all of these things, but her power is in the preciousness of God. A kingdom woman knows who she is, and she has a quiet beauty that can calm the wildest beast in a man or exert influence over many people and situations in ways that defy logic.

Because of Her Grace and Poise

It is very rare for my wife to accompany me when I travel to meet a ministry commitment because we decided that our children would be covered by at least one of us most of the time. On the occasions when she is able to travel with me, I am amazed by the response we receive! It reminds me of the time the late President John F. Kennedy noticed that whenever his gracious wife, Jacqueline, accompanied him on official trips, all of the attention seemed to gravitate to her. He quipped to the press, "I'm the one who's accompanying Jackie Kennedy."

My wife seems to take all of the attention when she travels with me, but it isn't because she *tries* to capture attention or force her way to the forefront. It is all because of her grace and poise and her generous support of me as her husband. Every time I take her with me, the host pastors take time to say, "Well, we know we are going to have a great service tonight because the First Lady and wife of Bishop Long is here with us tonight."

I'll never forget the time I was doing a book-signing promotion for my first book, *Taking Over,* at a Berean bookstore. The line of people waiting for me to sign their books stretched outside the building and around the corner. About an hour after the event began, my lovely wife made a quiet entrance and sat beside me at the table. Immediately, people began asking *her* to sign their books too.

Within fifteen or twenty minutes, my line had shifted over, and I watched in amazement while my wife signed my books—and *I* was the author! Her quiet grace, poise, and charm had literally won the hearts of the people there without any fanfare.

Finally, I had to whisper in her ear that she should probably leave so I could fulfill the publisher's request and promote the book myself—since I was the author.

SHE CAN BRING GOD'S PEACE ON THE SCENE

What a man really wants is a kingdom woman, a woman of wisdom. Kingdom women don't have to say a whole lot of words, although they are well able to do so. They don't have to argue and fuss, although most women can out-argue most men hands down. A wise woman of the kingdom knows there's a certain way she can stroke a man and speak into his heart that brings God's peace on the scene.

A kingdom woman, a wise woman, will tell you there's a particular way to deal with a man in nonconfrontational quietness that will have him "eating out of her hands." It is the tool God personally plants in kingdom women to help them build up kingdom men through quietness.

We have too many Christian women trying to fight a flesh war when God did not tell them to do that. That may explain why so many Christian marriages have ended in bitter divorce in recent years.

Am I saying those women were wrong and their husbands were 100 percent right? Absolutely not! Nobody is perfect, so no man is right all of the time (most hope to be right at least some of the time). That means every married couple will face conflict on a regular basis.

The Worst Thing a Woman Can Do

The problem isn't the conflict; the problem is the method used to address the issue. The worst thing a woman can do is "get in a man's face" as if she were a man. Everything in his mental, physical, and hormonal makeup is telling him to treat this beautiful attacker as he would another male.[3] If he is godly enough to know that isn't right, then he has only one choice. Walk away and stay away. Yet that choice is anti-kingdom as well!

What did God say about Adam in the Garden? Let's get His exact words to avoid any hint of human interference:

> The LORD God took the man and put him in the garden
> of Eden to tend and keep it. And the LORD God *commanded*

the man, saying, "Of every tree of the garden you may freely eat; but of the tree of the knowledge of good and evil you shall not eat, for in the day that you eat of it you shall surely die." And the LORD God said, *"It is not good that man should be alone;* I will *make him a helper comparable to him."* (Gen. 2:15–18, emphasis mine)

First, God gave Adam *instructions* about the tending, proper use, divine order, and prohibitions of the Garden. Then He said, "It is not good that man should be alone," and announced He would "make [Adam] a *helper* comparable to him." I see no mention of God creating an aggressor or adversary for Adam (there already was a garden snake fitting that description).

GOD BROUGHT IN THE HELPER, AND THE REST IS HUMAN HISTORY

Only after Adam had named and classified all of the species in the Garden did God decide it was time to provide that custom-designed helper He had promised to Adam. The rest is human history.

God was basically saying, "Man, you ain't gonna get this done without help, so I'm gonna bring you help." That's the order in the kingdom book—it had very little to do with "culture" because human culture didn't exist yet. That only happened after man sinned and his rebellious nature could no longer function in God's pure kingdom culture.

Kingdom men are looking for kingdom women who *like*

working together as a team in mutual dependence and kingdom order without strife and striving for superior position.

Did you notice a sense of awkwardness come over you when this subject came up? God isn't awkward about it, but we are. We are "modern" people after all—or are we? It seems to me our boast should be in our King and His kingdom rather than in our culture and man's supposed advancements. No human culture can hope to compete with the purity, joy, and empowerment available from the eternal kingdom culture.

Yet we wonder why men are turned off or driven away by smart women without wisdom who tell the men in their lives, "I've got a job—it's better than yours. I can buy my own food, and unlike you, I can cook it too. I can pay for the rent and buy my own car because I'm smart. What do I need you for?"

You May Not Need Me, but I Need You

God has called kingdom men to be humble men, so a humble man must reply to a smart woman:

"You may not need me, but I need you. When you declare your independence from me based on some economic advantage you enjoy, it implies that I have abused my authority to provide for, care for, love, and teach you what I have been taught.

"I'm supposed to be providing for you, but you disarmed me as a man and left me by the wayside in your quest for something that God never gave you. (He gave you something far better in my eyes—all of your knowledge is good, but I would prefer wisdom over mere knowledge.) All that you've acquired and achieved is good, but you were created to help me and stand *with* me—not *over* me."

Smart women often aren't wise enough to know that life with a "drone" isn't half as exciting as life with a real man. Why settle for a male who lives and thinks like a spiritually and emotionally castrated eunuch when you can live with a virile king and kingdom gentleman?

DESIGNED TO TEND AND CARE FOR GOD'S TREASURES

Like it or not, men were designed by God to tend and take care of God's treasures. Even ungodly men have the instinct of the Garden. If all the women are "independent" and unwise, then the men will feel driven to find somebody else to tend. Men who don't feel needed or respected tend to disintegrate from the inside out if they don't know who they are in Christ.

If you are a single woman and you don't want to help your man, then don't marry him. If you want a real man, then understand that a real man by divine order must take care of you.

There is only one person on this earth who can kill a man's spirit, and that is the woman that man is in love with. How can that be? God gave Eve and every woman after her an incredibly strong fighting spirit that is specifically aimed at the forces of Satan, the arch-adversary of womanhood, the womb, and the holy seed God sent through the human womb.

A Prophetic Impartation of
Spiritual Intensity and Ferocity

That is why a woman can pray so much better than most men. She instinctively understands the strategies of spiritual warfare through prayer. Once again, this impartation of spiritual intensity and ferocity can be traced directly to God's prophecy over Eve in the Garden:

> I will put enmity [hostility and hatred]
> Between you [Satan] and the woman,
> And between your seed and her Seed;
> He shall bruise your head,
> And you shall bruise His heel. (Gen. 3:15)

A kingdom man wants to hook up with a genuine kingdom woman who understands quietness, because a smart woman without wisdom doesn't understand or care that she possesses so much artillery in her spirit that what she says goes straight to a man's heart.

The first time a woman says she doesn't need the man God places in her life, she has killed his desire to take care of her. From that point on, about the only thing holding them together is sex or temporary economic advantage.

On the other hand, many married men know what they want, but they won't accept the responsibility to keep things hot on the home front. My stance on it is simple: In God's kingdom, the man is responsible for *everything*. That includes personal discipline and health maintenance.

If things have slowed down in the bedroom, have you asked yourself whether you are spending too much time inside the refrigerator or lounging in front of the television watching football and basketball games?

Are you lazy? You don't need that junk. Does she look at you and involuntarily say, "E-w-w. Don't touch me"? Work on that body, and give your wife something to work with.

HEY, MISTER: LEAVE THE BISCUIT ALONE

You've got too much over here and too little working over there. Lift and fold; stretch and go. Peel yourself off that sofa, and stop loafing. Get up in the morning, and make sure you leave the biscuit alone.

Work out, run, and push hard to make her look at you with admiration instead of overcoming faith. Make the investment in yourself so you can give *her* something to be proud of. She made a lifelong commitment to be true to you and you alone. Don't make her feel as if she is trapped in a lifelong nightmare of expanding waist sizes and spiraling cholesterol counts.

If you are single, you should know that dating is basically unbiblical, and it generally has the fruit to prove it. Nevertheless, I am well aware that many—if not most—single Christians do date. Unfortunately, the name of Jesus and the issues of His kingdom rarely come up when people date today. There are a lot of church folk on the dating circuit who prefer to launch a date with a kingdom phrase such as, "What's your sign?"

A kingdom man isn't (or shouldn't be) content to hook up

with an outwardly beautiful woman. He is really waiting for a single Christian woman whose inward development and godly worth show even more than her outward beauty. When a man meets a godly woman, he needs to see fruit from her inner life.

God has called every true man and woman of God to do "the work of ministry." We like to believe we hire professional folks to handle all of that, but the Bible says people like me are supposed to *equip* the people of the kingdom—all of the people—for kingdom work (Eph. 4:11–12). That should strongly influence the thinking and choices of every kingdom man who is considering marriage to a godly woman.

I wasn't looking when my time came. During my first four years as the pastor at New Birth, I was happily and busily single. I told the Lord, "I'm not going to date anybody at New Birth. I just don't want to deal with that. I guess I'm going to be single all my life."

Once I took down my "single and searching" sign, He *brought* Vanessa to me. Notice that I didn't say I *found* her or *looked* for her. God literally *brought* her to me, just as He brought Eve to Adam and Ruth to Boaz.

At the time, I was sitting at the Supreme Fish restaurant in downtown Atlanta just minding my own business when God delivered my wife special delivery and paraded her past the window. As soon as I saw Vanessa, I said, "Bone!"

· *Chapter 2* ·

WHAT DO YOU BELIEVE?

Your belief is magnetic. In fact, what you believe literally becomes your reality. If you believe a lie, then you may find your life entangled in an unending web of untruth, disappointment, and sorrow.

If you believe the truth, no matter how politically incorrect or unfashionable it may seem, then overall you will enjoy the obvious benefits of truth and godly hopes fulfilled.

IS IT GOD'S TRUTH OR A LIE DRESSED FOR CHURCH?

Human belief is so magnetic that once we choose to believe something, it draws to us those things we believe. It will also cause us to ignore all other information or facts that are inconsistent with those beliefs.

Be careful about what you believe. What do you believe about people? What do you believe about the Church and God's kingdom? Do you know why you are here?

If you believe your birth was an unwanted "accident," then you will look at yourself as a throwaway or disposable saint. What do you believe? Is it God's truth or a lie dressed for church?

Perhaps the most dangerous problem facing the body of Christ is our wholesale misunderstanding of biblical relationships between men and women. In fact, erroneous foundations of what constitutes a "real man" and a "real woman" plague most of the homes and marriages in God's kingdom. Men and women in the church just don't know how to work together to form a kingdom family.

We've freely mixed some biblical beliefs with our erroneous man-based beliefs, and they are drawing certain things to us that have nothing to do with God. Yet we think it's good. We justify our unbiblical and unspiritual beliefs and call them "spiritual" because so many other people in the church share those same erroneous beliefs.

We should just face the fact that God did *not* set up the church as a democracy. He didn't call for any vote to confirm whether or not His Word is true. It's *true* regardless of what we think about it. The majority does *not* rule in God's kingdom—that is one of those "man things" we *added* to the Word and called it holy.

Only God and His order rule in God's kingdom. Unfortunately, it takes a real man and a real woman to stand for the truth and resist wrong beliefs. As we shall see, real kingdom men and women seem to be in short supply at the moment.

Why do we need to talk about beliefs in a book about what a man wants and what a woman needs? Our beliefs about what makes a male a man and what makes a female a woman affect every area of life.

Once we decide what we believe, we tend to become set like concrete under a hot summer sun. If you don't stay tender before the Holy Spirit, you may become so hardened that you won't be open to change. You will refuse to hear anything that sounds new or fresh because it seems inconsistent with what you believe. My friend Randall Worley states that we are so afraid of being deceived, we close ourselves off from any new revelation.

OVERCOMING THE MIND-SET OF DISTRUST

I had the opportunity of working with a troubled young man who ultimately became one of my spiritual sons. He loved God more fervently than nearly anyone I knew, yet he had a rough side to his personality that seemed to offend many of the people around him.

God showed me his heart, and I realized that he had gone through great pain because of the rejection he felt from his father and others in his life. He didn't graduate from high school. On the last day of his senior year, he learned that he didn't have the necessary credits. He dreamed of becoming an NBA basketball star, but he knew he was going nowhere without a high-school diploma. By the time we met, he was heartbroken and had a great mistrust for anyone in authority.

He seemed to do well under my mentorship, becoming a teacher, then a minister, and finally an elder in the church. He had "caught my spirit" so well that he effectively taught the truth and shared the Word with many in the congregation and the city. Yet I learned later that in spite of his success, he had never received the truth in his own life.

I decided to take him with me on a ministry trip to Dallas, Texas, and Detroit, Michigan. One night I said, "Listen, we're going to talk all night if we have to because something has to change in you so you can become more trusting toward others. If you ever deal with this, God will use you in a mighty way."

We talked all night and went to breakfast the next morning. All of a sudden, the truth finally broke through the core of his cemented mind-set like a jackhammer breaking through concrete. Everything loosened up, and his stony heart was transformed into a fleshly heart that was pliable in God's hand.

He understood that he didn't have to fight to survive anymore. By God's grace, he was no longer on the bottom. He had been lifted to the top and was seated high.

I remember the day we returned to Atlanta. Everyone in the office noticed how much this young man had changed. He was open, loving, and consistently happy.

Later on, this young man was playing basketball with some of the men at a men's advance and suddenly collapsed after suffering a fatal heart attack.

This man had one of the largest home-goings of any one of our church members, and it was because he had helped so many people. Although this man died in his twenties, I was blessed to see a person who had been so stuck in his ways because of rejection throughout his early life overcome it all in

Christ. He received the truth from God's Word and pressed through to become a blessing to many others before his earthly life ended.

I'm convinced that *all* of us have wrong mind-sets that must be broken up and replaced with truth from God's Word, even if we don't have the difficult background this young man had.

Why do so many people file into America's churches Sunday after Sunday, sing some songs, hear a sermon, and go home *unchanged, unchallenged,* and *unconvinced* that God has called them to *more?*

Left to ourselves, we tend to draw to our hearts only the things we already believe (or *want* to believe). We refuse to be challenged by new revelation or new applications of old revelation—we want to hear things that will support our beliefs and coddle our compulsion to seek comfort. Frankly, this book almost certainly will challenge some of the politically correct beliefs you have about dating and marriage relationships. But the concepts I am presenting aren't based on human opinion or cultural patterns. They comprise a prescription for kingdom order and peace on earth based on God's unchanging Word.

On a personal basis, you and I instinctively go to great lengths to avoid a challenge to our status quo. If we aren't careful, we will bypass any viewpoint from a different angle (so much for the ministries of John the Baptist, Jesus Christ, and the apostle Paul). Then we want to whine and complain and cry on Pastor's shoulder because we've been passed over for recognition as mature leaders in the body of Christ.

STUCK IN A FLESH-BASED PARADIGM

Honestly, the only thing that should be "recognized" about most of us when we miss an opportunity to grow in Christ is that we are stuck in a flesh-based paradigm of our own making. It all goes back to our refusal to hear God speaking in a new way.

Only set in concrete those things that God declares are fixed and unchanging. That includes our fundamental understanding of marriage and human relationships as revealed in His Word. It does *not* include cultural peculiarities, local religious customs, or personal opinions and practices in local church settings not specifically spelled out in God's Word.

I love the local church. I pastor a local church, but there is something far larger in the cosmos than any local church—it is the eternal *kingdom* of God. The only way to step into God's purposes and blessings is to lay down our personal agendas and be conformed to the image of our King, the Lord Jesus Christ.

Many of us struggle to remain in terrible marriage relationships because we go at it with *our* ideas when *God's* vision of marriage in His kingdom is usually totally different from ours. He has provided specific guidelines for the roles, relationships, and responsibilities of men and women in the kingdom. If we ever hope to get back on God's track again, then we have to go about it God's way. Let me say it right up front: It's better to teach and preach what God says and live that way than to live the way you see fit and edit God's Word accordingly.

If we don't understand ourselves in Christ, we will walk in the flesh and not in the Spirit. That isn't a new revelation by any means, but the problem is made far worse when we parade our way through life *thinking and pretending that we are in the Spirit.* Pardon my slang, but we ain't in the Spirit. "We be in the flesh, flesh, flesh."

This kind of erroneous thinking produces deadly and deep-seated selfishness and self-righteousness that permeate everything in our lives. This is the bottom line: Our attempts to satisfy our selfish wants without God have produced the incredible mess we have today.

Somewhere in our lives, in our minds, or in our spirits, we somehow got ahead of God with our wants and desires. Our selfish determination to get what we want *now* got so bad that we decided to go around God. "Why not?" we ask. "He is just taking too long with this thing. He obviously needs some help."

Nobody bothered to consult with Sarah and Abraham about the mess they produced by trying to "help God." They died thousands of years ago in a land thousands of miles and entire cultures removed from us, yet we are still paying a bloody price for their impatient "solution" to "God's problem."[1]

Did you ever get in the car-pool lane and somebody's going slow? It gives you a new appreciation for patience, doesn't it? That's God. You're trying to get around all the traffic to get where you're going—all because you overslept. Now God's in the fast lane going slow, and you're cussing God.

For people who should know better, we get into way too much trouble because of our lust. What is lust? Lust is our desire to have what we want *now,* regardless of the consequences. Obviously, this includes sexual desires and appetites, but it really includes every area of life. What are *you* trying to get now at any cost?

Are you trying to buy something that you don't really need?

("But I just gotta have it. I want it. I mean, I *r-e-a-l-l-y* want it.")

What about your mortgage payment? ("I'll take care of that later. Right now, I want that *thing* and I'm gonna get it, no matter what.")

ASK GOD ABOUT THE *WHY* BEHIND YOUR WANT

You're in lust. Wait for the want, and pay for your need first. Then ask God about the *why* behind your want. Make sure it is part of God's kingdom plan for your life. Will that boat become the idol you worship on Sundays when you should be worshiping the one true God? Will that man or woman become your partner in the kingdom or your burden from hell?

You can't answer that question until you can answer this one: Do you know who you are? Your understanding of yourself depends on what you think and believe about God and His purpose for your life.

If your understanding of yourself is based on how you think and your thinking is wrong, then what happens once you set your beliefs in the concrete of human pride and self-centeredness? You tend to ignore anything that seems inconsistent with your belief.

In King Asa's day, ancient Israel had been divided into two nations, Israel and Judah. By the time young King Asa ascended to the throne of Judah, the country had deteriorated into an atheist nation under the corrupt leadership of his deceased father, King Abijam, and Asa's grandmother, Queen Maachah.

King Asa did his best to "buck the tide" and lead his nation back to God. The first thing: He had to remove the wrong foundations.

He replaced them with the right belief in the true God, with God's law or order, and with godly teaching priests who would help the people replace their wrong beliefs with truth.

Judah faced virtual extinction in the Old Testament after a godly king named Asa dared to stand up for God and His kingdom against impossible odds. When a million-man Ethiopian army came against them, King Asa cried out to God, and He miraculously delivered His people.

Then God sent a prophet to bring encouragement and specific direction to Asa. He spoke to the king of Judah as if that remnant nation represented the reunited split kingdom (comprising both Israel and Judah): "For a long time Israel has been without *the true God,* without a *teaching priest,* and *without law;* but when in their trouble they turned to the LORD God of Israel, and sought Him, He was found by them" (2 Chron. 15:3–4, emphasis mine).

Israel was laboring along under the weight of a threefold lie when the prophet came along with this word of correction and hope. How many marriages and relationships in the church face the same problems today?

WE WOULD RATHER LIVE WITH
A LIE THAN GET RIGHT

We are so arrogant and stuck in our pride that we would rather live with a lie than humble ourselves and get right with God. It is time to admit something is wrong and humbly pray, "God, teach us."

When we choose to follow our flesh, we don't know what we're

Prov 29:18

going to be like from day to day—it all seems to change with the latest things we crave.

You cannot have a kingdom without a king. The king—not the citizens of the realm—dictates the laws and the statutes of the kingdom. We *believe* we have all the rights and privileges of first-class voting citizens in this kingdom, but we've failed to listen to our King. He says, "My kingdom is not a democracy; there are no votes here." God didn't establish His kingdom to please or serve us; He established the kingdom for His pleasure, and we live to serve and worship Him.

You may disagree with me (and that is okay), but I am convinced that every church that "votes" on matters of the Spirit and supernatural calling is out of order. You cannot vote on something decreed, imparted, and empowered by God.

Now for the disconcerting revelation driving the passion behind this book: I want to suggest to you that many of us *have never seen a real woman or a real man.* Perhaps most of us don't even know what we're looking for!

I have been called to lay a foundation within the body of Christ of the kingdom. That means I am called to till or plow up the crusty ground. To be honest, I'm determined to upset you because the Father is upsetting me for a divine purpose.

DETERIORATING FROM THE INSIDE OUT

Any created being begins to deteriorate from the inside out when he is missing *the Creator, the one true God.* This problem plagued ancient Israel, and it is a problem threatening the modern church.

When God began to deal with me about His kingdom, I realized that I wasn't going to be very popular in the years ahead (as many as God gives me on this earth). Why? I realized that the local church represents the kingdom of the true God. That means we must avoid all appearance of evil in our conduct and representation of the kingdom to the world (1 Thess. 5:22).

When my church was asked to participate in an event labeled "The Million-Family March," we knew our refusal would not be well received by the Black Muslim sponsors of the event. However, we could not in good conscience be party to something that would confuse people. If you watched the event on television as a Christian or as someone seeking the truth about Christ, you would be confused about the identity of the true King because there was so much of a mixture.

Many churches chose to support the event, but there was a great risk of planting confusion in the hearts of casual viewers, the everyday folks in barbershops, shopping malls, and manufacturing plants who wondered, "Who is the one true God? Is this trick or treat—pick your favorite flavor, any one will do?"

Do You Live As If God Is Dead?

If we examine the fruit on the tree of the American church scene, we must conclude that many of us are tied up in the spirit of antichrist. How can that be? We really don't believe in and serve a true God. We have conformed the church to the image of our own beliefs and ended up with a social outlet rather than a place of submission to the King. Therefore, we are atheists in mind because we *believe* and act as if it is all right to do with Him as we please. This has had a devastating effect on our marriages, our homes, and our children.

We skillfully confuse the issue even further in the body of Christ by pretending to do whatever the King requests us to do— *as long as the requests conform to our preset belief system.* Anything outside that narrow circle of our personal approval—especially anything related to "dirty words" such as *respect, honor,* and *submission*—is minimized, exorcised, cauterized, or vaporized.

We hide our ruthless editing of God's Word, using phrases such as "These things passed away with the first-century apostles" or "That was Old Testament" or "That was then, this is now—things are different in the modern era."

That means the first things to hit the editing floor are especially offensive and "narrow-minded" passages such as these:

> I testify to everyone who hears the words of the prophecy of this book: If anyone adds to these things, God will add to him the plagues that are written in this book; and if anyone takes away from the words of the book of this prophecy, God shall take away his part from the Book of Life, from the holy city, and from the things which are written in this book. (Rev. 22:18–19)

> All Scripture is given by inspiration of God, and is profitable for doctrine, for reproof, for correction, for instruction in righteousness, that the man of God may be complete, thoroughly equipped for every good work . . .

Preach the word! Be ready in season and out of season. Convince, rebuke, exhort, with all longsuffering and teaching. For the time will come when they will not endure sound doctrine, but according to their own desires, because they have itching ears, they will heap up for themselves teachers; and they will turn their ears away from the truth, and be turned aside to fables. (2 Tim. 3:16–17; 4:2–4)

We joyfully call Him "Lord" as long as He is feeding us, blessing us, or answering our prayers. We rebuke the devil and disregard His Word and His ministers whenever He requires us to do something or trust Him for something outside our belief systems or comfort zones. If He is truly Lord, our only answer in every situation is *yes!*

If I asked you to go to the bank and withdraw a million dollars using my name, you would probably obey my request with joy. (If you wouldn't, there would probably be several thousand waiting anxiously in the line behind you who would.) Would that act of obedience mean that I am "Lord" over your life? Hardly. It simply means I offered enough personal incentive to encourage you in your personal pursuit of pleasure or gain.

HOW ABOUT THAT CRUCIFIXION SERVICE?

We could easily have the largest service in our ministry's history if I announced a "Debt-Cancellation Service," but the numbers would be significantly lower if I announced a "Kingdom Crucifixion-of-the-Flesh Service" for the following Sunday. Do you wonder why?

If we judge ourselves by the fruit of our lives, then the body of Christ has an atheist spirit in thought and practical function. All outward evidence indicates we really don't believe what we say we believe. There is truth to the old axiom, "Actions speak louder than words."

Whether we jump and holler and shout pious platitudes in every church service or conduct religious performances in somber services with kneelers and prayer books, we are in trouble if our actions throughout the week shout to the world from the highest rooftops, "God really isn't God!"

The people of Judah before King Asa's reforms were still tending the sacrificial fires of empty religion. Some of the priests were still making sacrifices in the temple, and the sacrificial fires were still smoldering, but Israel had lost the true view of God. They put most of their affections on the idols and false gods that pandered to their flesh the best.

Serving the God in a Box

The inhabitants of Judah wanted a convenient God. By definition, a convenient or comfortable god is a deity whom you could control. It is a lot like serving the god in a box, the one who pops up at your command and disappears from sight just as quickly.

"Bishop, isn't this book supposed to be about what a man wants and what a woman needs? I'm ready to get to the good stuff."

There is no way you will listen to what God has to say about "the good stuff" of manhood and womanhood in the kingdom unless you are willing to submit yourself to the King.

If the King and His kingdom don't interest you, then perhaps you are better off hangin' with the talk-show queens and shock-show kings of daily television who will cater to your every whim.

If you don't get your King right, then you won't listen to anything I have to say because I'm out to build and establish the kingdom of God in the earth of men.

God is looking for a true church, not a social gathering of hypocrites. Either we acknowledge Him as God and King, or we take down every cross and remove His name from every sign, door, and doorpost—or else be accused of false advertisement.

No, I believe Joshua said it best:

> If it seems evil to you to serve the LORD, *choose for yourselves this day whom you will serve,* whether the gods which your fathers served that were on the other side of the River, or the gods of the Amorites, in whose land you dwell. *But as for me and my house, we will serve the LORD.* (Josh. 24:15, emphasis mine)

WELCOME TO THE MUSEUM OF REAL KINGDOM PEOPLE

Since I've already gone too far, I should say what I'm really thinking much of the time. The missing element of the kingdom is real men and real women of the King. My secret suspicion is that this element is so rare that once we find the real thing, we really need to build a museum and display a real kingdom man and a real kingdom woman.

Why am I so fervent about this? I'm convinced that every day we embrace the false and the unbiblical in place of godly womanhood and manhood, we continue to curse generation after generation to the horror of living a lie.

The real challenge of embracing God's idea of our true roles and responsibilities is that nobody seems to know how a real man looks and lives! No one knows how a true woman looks and lives either. We are all running around conducting "experiments" and making unauthorized modifications to God's original formula, and our man-made creations and concoctions are blowing up in our "laboratories."

I believe that there are two keys to right living in God's kingdom. You must *think* right and *feel* right to live right before God. Our King never said life in His kingdom would be automatic or naturally easy. He did have something to say about the subject, however. This is what the King said about embracing the challenges of kingdom life: "Take My yoke upon you and learn from Me, for I am gentle and lowly in heart, and you will find rest for your souls. For My yoke is easy and My burden is light" (Matt. 11:29–30).

The first step to success in the kingdom is to make a choice—to step under His yoke *by choice* and *learn* from Him. Israel's problems (and the problems of the modern church) arose because there was no true God, no teaching priest, and no law. The church seems to be awash in a sea of empty and vain thoughts.

THINK WORLDLY, LIVE GODLY?

Oswald Chambers said, "We are taught to think like pagans and to live as Christians." In essence, we are taught to *think* in the flesh or to *think worldly* through life but somehow *live godly*. We can't have it both ways. We know that "a double-minded man

[is] unstable in all his ways" (James 1:8). That's an unfortunately accurate assessment of the modern church. The Bible declares that as a man "thinks in his heart, so is he" (Prov. 23:7). Jesus said, "A good man out of the good treasure of his heart brings forth good; and an evil man out of the evil treasure of his heart brings forth evil. For *out of the abundance of the heart his mouth speaks"* (Luke 6:45, emphasis mine).

Worldly thinking and godly living are totally incompatible. They are mutually exclusive terms—in other words, they don't get along, and they don't mix without disastrous results.

The dangers of the double-minded life became a major focus of the apostle James later in his life. Perhaps he knew the true meaning of the compound Greek word *dipsuchos,* translated as "double-minded" in English. It means "two-spirited, i.e., vacillating (in opinion or purpose):—double minded."[2]

"Two-spirited" people try to straddle the dividing line between darkness and light, the invisible boundary between the created world (*kosmos*) and the eternal kingdom of God. This impossible spiritual gymnastic feat produces only instability. James summarized God's cure for man's disease when he said:

> Adulterers and adulteresses! Do you not know that friendship with the world is enmity with God? *Whoever therefore wants to be a friend of the world makes himself an enemy of God.* Or do you think that the Scripture says in vain, "The Spirit who dwells in us yearns jealously"? But He gives more grace. Therefore He says:
>
> "God resists the proud,

But gives grace to the humble."

Therefore submit to God. Resist the devil and he will flee from you. Draw near to God and He will draw near to you. *Cleanse your hands, you sinners; and purify your hearts, you double-minded.* (James 4:4–8, emphasis mine)

The only way to leave behind what is wrong is to discover what is right. We must discover what it means to be a part of God's kingdom.

· *Chapter 3* ·

WHAT A WOMAN NEEDS

G od the Creator and the women He created share something in common—they need men.

Not just any men will do—they need kingdom men. It could
be discouraging for the women of the kingdom if God wasn't
involved in the hunt, but He is. A woman might be depressed if
she believed all of the statistics about mismatched male-female
ratios and the rising singles population in many areas of the
United States.

Things look even worse when she elevates her standards
beyond the singles bar minimum requirement that the man be
breathing and have most of his equipment in working order.

Once a woman realizes that she needs nothing less than a
kingdom man, the search mission appears to become a miracle
hunt. In the minds of many, the effort would seem hopeless
except for one all-important detail: She has stepped into God's
divine order and perfect will.

If you trust Him, He obligates Himself to work on your

behalf. Once you step into the right place in His kingdom, when you get right, then God's got something for you. He will create a man for a trusting kingdom woman if necessary; He will supply her need.

Some women in the church will tell you, "No, I don't want that. I've been there, done that, don't want that." I respect their personal opinions, but I have to say they've probably been at the wrong place. I wonder if they have hooked up with kingdom men or experienced relationship the kingdom way. Once that happens, I'm convinced they wouldn't want anything less because that is God's kingdom plan and order.

God declared through the prophet Jeremiah, "I beheld, and indeed there was no man" (Jer. 4:25). Even in this Bible passage, God wasn't looking for just any old male; He was searching for a *real man* who could be found faithful to the Lord.

At the Brink of Destruction, God Searched for a Man

It seems the whole world is in desperate need of genuine kingdom men, almost as if the future depends on it. It does. When sin took Jerusalem to the brink of destruction in Jeremiah's time, God was searching for a kingdom man:

> Run to and fro through the streets of Jerusalem;
> See now and know;
> And seek in her open places
> *If you can find a man,*

If there is anyone who executes judgment,
Who seeks the truth,
And I will pardon her. (Jer. 5:1, emphasis mine)

Why are church people so consumed with problems in relationships? It is because no one is secure in who he or she is. Men don't know what real men are, and women don't know how to be real women.

Our churches are filled with people who surround themselves with defensive walls and "pretend" personalities. They fear the day someone actually discovers who they really are and how they really feel. To me, that sounds like a good description of hell on earth.

We live in a backward society that calls good evil and evil good. It bases its opinions and laws on the whim of the moment and ever-shifting pockets of political power, and it wonders why everything keeps getting worse from generation to generation. The reason is simple: All true government authority stems from the authority and inviolate laws of God and the King.

WON'T ANY MALE WITH MACHO DO?

In the middle of all this mess, women, especially godly women, are searching for kingdom men. What is so special about a kingdom man? Won't any male with macho do?

A kingdom man understands that he will never be what he is supposed to be without a kingdom woman. He understands that his manhood is wrapped up in her womanhood and vice versa.

If we start going our separate ways (as men and women), we

will never rule and have dominion in the earth. We need each other according to the agenda of God, and any other concept or doctrine is a trick from the devil. (The truth is that if we don't get with the agenda of God, we will all die in this miserable, lonely, destitute state that we're in right now. I'm convinced that because of human agendas, most of the people in any given public gathering—including church—are lonely.)

What a woman needs is a praying man. Paul the apostle said, "I desire therefore that the men pray everywhere, lifting up holy hands, without wrath and doubting" (1 Tim. 2:8). A true man of God prays. He isn't content to sit around year after year and rely on his wife or the women in the church to do all the praying.

A genuine kingdom man rises early to seek the face of God. He knows how to lift his hands in prayer. He knows how to bow to the ground in humility and call on the name of the Lord. A real man prays without ceasing because he knows it is one of the vital secrets to his power and authority in the earth.

IT'S GOD'S WORD—POLITICALLY CORRECT OR NOT

Godly women need men who have their priorities in kingdom order. Godly men understand that whether God's Word is politically correct or not at the moment, it still says:

> For man is not from woman, but woman from man. *Nor was man created for the woman,* but woman for the man. For this reason the woman ought to have a symbol of authority on her head, because of

the angels. Nevertheless, neither is man independent of woman, nor woman independent of man, in the Lord. For as woman came from man, even so man also comes through woman; but all things are from God. (1 Cor. 11:8–12, emphasis mine)

Men who believe they were "made for the woman" will be tempted to place the will of their wives over the will of God. Those who know better understand that they were made to conquer the earth, establish the kingdom, and tend the treasures of God. Chief among those treasures are the kingdom women in their lives and the children of God they bring into the earth.

GOD NEVER GAVE MAN A FINISHED PRODUCT

Another characteristic of a kingdom man is his careful attention to what I call *cultivation*. He understands that God has never given man a finished product. Adam was placed in a Garden that needed tending. Abraham was given a promise that demanded years of faithfulness to trigger its fulfillment. Moses was given an assignment and a rod—the rest would come about only through hard work and ever-expanding faith.

Believe it or not, God requires a kingdom man to cultivate everything and everyone He places in his life. That specifically includes the woman he marries and any children they have.

"Where did you come up with that foolishness, Bishop?"

I'm glad you asked, but you should have asked Dr. Jesus and Reverend Paul. In the book of Ephesians, Paul made it clear that

Jesus set the eternal standard and high mark for all kingdom men:

> Husbands, love your wives, just as Christ also loved the church and gave Himself for her, that He might *sanctify* and *cleanse her* with the *washing of water by the word,* that He might present her to Himself a glorious church, not having spot or wrinkle or any such thing, but *that she should be holy and without blemish.* So husbands ought to love their own wives as their own bodies; he who loves his wife loves himself. For no one ever hated his own flesh, but nourishes and cherishes it, just as the Lord does the church. For we are members of His body, of His flesh and of His bones. "For this reason a man shall leave his father and mother and be joined to his wife, and the two shall become one flesh." (Eph. 5:25–31, emphasis mine)

Paul added the detailed application to the marriage relationship when he stated, "Nevertheless let each one of you in particular so love his own wife as himself, and let the wife see that she respects her husband. Children, obey your parents in the Lord, for this is right" (Eph. 5:33–6:1). Notice that the husband is to love his wife and the wife is to respect her husband. This is a major side point.

We Rush in with Erasers Where Angels Don't Dare to Tread

Kingdom order resonates throughout these Bible passages, but too many of us rush in with erasers where angels don't dare to tread. We want to rewrite, abridge, and "correct" the Word of God to conform to the cockeyed, relativistic gender roles that have dominated our media and Western culture over the last thirty years.

God expects every husband to do for his wife what Jesus Christ did for the church: to *sanctify* and *cleanse her* with the *washing of water by the Word.* When a man marries a woman, he accepts the responsibility to "sanctify" her or "set her apart as holy" in the order of the kingdom. It is his responsibility to use the revelation of God's Word to show her who she is and call her into her destiny. His job is to help her step into everything God has ordained for her life.

A kingdom woman wants a genuine kingdom man in her life because she needs his loving ministry in her life for completion (just as he needs her). Christ sanctifies the church, and a husband sanctifies his wife.

"So what about all of that man's *problems,* Bishop? How can I submit to *that* mess?"

In the first place, if you're single and you say you really want a godly man, then don't go up to him and say, "I'm a Leo. Are you a Cancer?" Ask him, "What is your understanding, biblically, about men and women? I'm trying to learn." See if the man knows God and studies His Word.

LOOK PAST THE PRETENDER AND SAY, "NEXT!"

If you are a single woman, don't get hooked up with some guy who quickly nods and says, "Yeah, I'm saved," but can't tell you what he was saved from. If he can't tell you how he got saved or outline the plan of salvation, then nod and look past the pretender while you say, "Next!"

If the man you married is considerably less than the man you thought you were getting, welcome to the club. None of us men are perfect, but we do respond to two great powers in the universe—the power of God and the considerable power He placed in godly women.

Don't get in your man's face and attempt to argue or wrestle him into the kingdom position. No, just pull out your *big* guns, the gifts God gave you for this very emergency. Assault the carnal-man mountain with your gentle spirit.

Use Encouragement Instead of Belittlement

All right, I know that there is a good chance the man doesn't even know the Lord's Prayer because you didn't check on that before you married him. By this time, he should have at least been exposed to it. Just find it in the Word for him, and put it in front of his face and press your case with encouragement instead of belittlement. Before long he'll just have to respond to your quiet spirit and irresistibly gentle approach.

Tools of Endearment: Beauty, Brilliance, Discernment, and Power

God gave women something powerful and effective. He gave them four powerful tools of endearment to the masculine heart:

beauty, brilliance, discernment, and the power to wrap men around their little fingers with their quiet spirits.

If you want your husband to become a kingdom man, make sure you use the womanly gifts God gave you to help move and motivate him into his calling in the kingdom. The greatest power a man has is his position and love. You cannot beat a man when it comes to loving, protecting, and tending.

When a man is in position in the kingdom, he exercises true authority and is a prophet, priest, and king in his home and in every area of his life. The more time he spends with God, the more God will speak to him about your needs, his responsibilities in the home and marriage, and the divine calling for everyone in the family. He will be able to speak destiny into your life and the lives of your children.

Remember that in God's kingdom, men and women are equal in essence but different in function. It has *nothing* to do with innate worth or ability. It has everything to do with order and personal responsibility to *submit* to authority and kingdom order.

EVERY GOOD GIFT IS TIED UP IN OUR SUBMISSION TO GOD'S ORDER

The subject of submission rarely comes up in genuinely godly homes because both marriage partners routinely submit *to each other*. We must understand that everything God wants to give us (whether we are male or female) is tied up in our submission and in our obedience to His order. Submission does not occur when you agree; it occurs when everything in you may disagree, yet you yield to God's authority.

All of this reinforces what I am about to say: A kingdom man always adds value to the woman he loves and marries. When a woman takes a man's name in marriage and submits to him as her husband, he is covering her with his own life, calling, reputation, and potential in Christ. He had better not drag her backward!

A young woman gives up the good name of her own father to receive the covering of her husband—so he is under an obligation of God to add value to her lifelong decision to stand with him.

The only way a man can add value is to acquire something worth contributing to her life. There is only one Source for that—God Himself. A kingdom man pays the price to learn and receive revelation from God so he can make a value-added deposit in his wife's life and calling.

Every kingdom woman really needs and deserves a kingdom man who knows his duty to be a pastor to "the church in his own home." He knows he is personally responsible to teach and "wash" his wife with the water of the Word. That means he needs to study to show himself approved (2 Tim. 2:15 KJV). If he doesn't, his brilliant wife just might show him up!

UNDERSTANDING: THE DIFFERENCE
BETWEEN SUCCESS AND FAILURE

A good woman needs a godly man who has understanding. It can make all the difference between success and failure in a Christian home and marriage! Consider these statements by the apostle Peter: "Husbands, likewise, dwell with them *with understanding,* giving *honor* to the wife, as to the weaker vessel, and as being heirs *together* of the grace of life, *that your prayers may not be hindered*" (1 Peter 3:7, emphasis mine).

This passage provides tremendous balance to the marriage relationship, and it does it with a stern warning none of us can afford to ignore. First, Peter told husbands to live with their wives "with understanding" or in an understanding way.

I would never presume to say any man totally understands a woman. The very mystery of a woman's complexity is part of her irresistible attraction. Men were formed from the dirt, but women were re-formed and further perfected by the hand of God. I doubt if men will ever fully understand women, and women will probably always be a step ahead of us in the understanding department. Nevertheless, God requires that men be understanding toward their wives.

Peter also commanded husbands to "honor" their wives. Most of us have no idea what the original Greek word translated as "honor" actually means. If we did, it might help solve most of the problems wives have with God's command to submit to their husbands. Peter used the Greek word *time* (pronounced "tee-may"), and it means "to give esteem of the highest degree, to give dignity itself" to someone.[1]

ARE YOUR PRAYERS BEING CUT DOWN, CUT OFF, OR CUT OUT?

The final segment of Peter's command is shocking. It may also explain why the prayers of so many people in the church appear to be powerless and useless. Peter warned hardheaded husbands that if they fail to show understanding and give esteem and dignity of the highest degree to their wives as equal partners in their kingdom inheritance, then *their prayers will be hindered.* The word translated "hindered" literally means "to cut down, cut off, or cut out."[2]

As for the woman who wants her husband to be a true kingdom man, her part is to resist the urge to "fix" her husband through her own efforts, arguments, and marital pressure. She can accomplish the same thing God's way by using her gift of a quiet and submissive spirit to lead her husband to his anointed position of destiny. The key is to "get out of the way" so the angels of God can deal with her husband on another level.

There is a good reason for a kingdom woman to desire a lifelong union with a kingdom man. When a man submits to the will of God and yields to the work of the Holy Spirit, God plants a unique ability in him to awaken the masculinity in a boy and release the femininity in a girl.

A godly mother nurtures these things with anointed ability, but a godly father can somehow speak them into existence and summon them into full bloom in the authority of his position. Ideally, it takes both anointings to properly carry a child to maturity in the kingdom of God.

The Only Way Hell Can Bother Us

It seems clear to me from the Scriptures that the only way hell can bother us is when we get out of position. God won't bless a mess, but He will move heaven and earth to bless and protect His children when they bow their knees and yield their wills to His.

If you are a kingdom woman in need of a kingdom man, take your stand for God today. Submit your life to Him and to those He has placed in authority, and put your trust in Him. Become a mother to the motherless right now, even though you are single. Plant a godly seed of nurture and anointed motherhood in the life of another today so God can deliver to you a harvest of motherhood tomorrow—with your own godly husband and the children of your womb.

Begin to pray today for the husband He will bring you in the days to come. Pray for those around you who also need a kingdom man in their lives; and pray for your married friends whose husbands still live far below their kingdom destiny.

Above all, don't drop your standards below His kingdom standard. No one in God's kingdom should settle for less than a kingdom spouse in his or her life. This reminds me of the way one young lady and her fiancé held the line for righteousness and refused to drop their standards under the pressure of temptation. Their story represents both a joy and a pain to me.

I am gratified that the members of my congregation receive me as their spiritual father. Many of them who were never fathered by their natural fathers especially receive me as a father in the ministry. This couple, in particular, yielded to the Word of God I ministered in our services. Both viewed me as their spiritual father although we never really spent time together.

Just before they were married, they expressed their gratitude to me for speaking to them as a father with a message of no compromise. Although they experienced the normal temptation young people face just before marriage, they walked out the truth of the Word, went through the premarital counseling we provide at New Birth, and remained sexually pure until their wedding night.

This couple had captured the truth that their wedding day was not the "pinnacle" of their married life; it was merely a foretaste and sample of the joy they would experience as their love and covenant commitment moved from glory to glory in the truth. (This was the joy of my story. My difficult schedule produced the pain I felt because I was unable to conduct their wedding ceremony as they desired.)

If you are a woman who is married to someone who does not belong to the kingdom, then pull out the big guns of a quiet spirit and a submissive heart. That apparently unmovable stone lounging in your living room and bedroom is about to come face-to-face with God's irresistible force. It isn't a contest.

SET LOOSE THE ANGELIC HOUNDS OF HEAVEN!

A man in the grip of his wife's quiet submission under God can run, but he cannot hide. By stepping aside in submission and quietness of spirit, a godly woman opens the door and "sets the angelic hounds of heaven" loose on her kingdom-husband construction project!

What does a woman want? Pastor Darlene Bishop, a wise kingdom woman, explained it this way to my congregation:

We just want to be held and caressed. We get married thinking that we want to be treated like a lady, held like a baby, and honored like your mama. And when we don't get that, sure we're disappointed . . .

The problem in most marriages today is that we don't communicate. We women need to communicate. When we scream at you because we've had to warm supper three times, we're not really mad because we had to warm up supper three times . . . we ain't been kissed in a *month*. But we got too much pride to tell ya.

To men, suggestions work better than direct orders. We need to realize that God made men and women different from one another for a divine purpose that also happens to be perfectly logical. We used to be together in one body—in Adam's body. The book of Genesis makes it clear that all we see in women today was extracted from Adam and re-formed in Eve in the beginning.

That implies at least three logical conclusions: (1) Men no longer have those qualities in and of themselves, (2) women do not possess all the qualities of manhood in and of themselves, and (3) men and women need one another to form the complete being God anointed to subdue the earth and establish His kingdom on earth.

EVEN THE SECULAR WORLD HAS DROPPED THE "UNISEX" FACADE

Why do we insist on adopting and enforcing the disproved 1960s "unisex" concept of gender (mal)function in the church and home? After decades of artificially promoting total equality of function and ability of men and women to children in the schools and to society as a whole, even the secular world has largely dropped the facade. This is particularly true in the areas of medical knowledge, psychological function, sociological relationships and responsibilities, and fashion and design.

Despite every effort of the feminist movement, women are beginning to force corporations to acknowledge the importance of the family. They are demanding innovative changes such as in-company child-care services, flextime work schedules, at-home offices, and other adaptations that allow them to fulfill their God-ordained roles as mothers—no matter how politically incorrect it was in the past.

Again, God's Word has declared since the beginning that men and women are *equal in essence* or innate value and *different in function.* It is a fact that men and women differ significantly in their hormonal makeup. They differ physiologically in areas related to reproduction, nurture, and methods of human interaction, yet they are so identical in other areas that medical doctors freely exchange the blood and vital organs of male and female donors in emergency situations.

What does a woman want? Deep down inside, where the foolish propaganda and popular cultural whims cannot reach, a woman needs a *real man.* She longs to be united with a man anointed of God to bring completion to her God-ordained destiny.

Salvation comes to each of us from Christ Jesus alone—whether we are male or female. But once we receive Him and submit to Him as King, our destiny is inevitably linked to our kingdom relationships with others.

Whether we approve of it or not, God has ordained that men and women in His kingdom unite in marriage to form godly families and birth new children into His kingdom.

God hasn't apologized for His decision yet, and He never will. That means we have two choices about the matter: We submit to His kingdom order and enjoy all of its benefits, or we rebel against God's order and suffer the consequences of going it on our own.

So what does a woman need? She needs a man—God's man. What does God look for when He wants to redeem nations and raise up God-fearing families? He looks for a man who will execute justice and seek truth. He looks for a kingdom man. If you are still waiting for a kingdom man to enter your life, trust God and release Him to search out a kingdom man for you too.

> In this manner, therefore, pray:
> Our Father in heaven,
> Hallowed be Your name.
> *Your kingdom come.*
> *Your will be done*
> *On earth* as it is in heaven. (Matt. 6:9–10, emphasis mine)

· *Chapter 4* ·

THE MISSING ELEMENT
OF THE KINGDOM

S omething is missing here. I just can't put my finger on it."
Several years ago, Hollywood released a movie about the workers in an American automobile-manufacturing plant after it was purchased by a Japanese automaker and placed under the control of a Japanese management team.

After a series of predictable and laughable confrontations between the rigid Japanese managers and unionized and independent-minded American autoworkers, the two groups reluctantly began to work together.

The catalyst for unity was survival: They had to produce a record number of cars before the president of the company arrived to inspect the plant. If they failed the test, the plant would be shut down, all of the workers would be laid off, and the Japanese managers would return home in shame.

Once the two warring parties decided to work together, they virtually worked a miracle by meeting the production goal.

Unfortunately, the last car had to be thrown together at high speed just before the president arrived.

When the inspection was complete, the president was about to praise the "odd-couple" manufacturing team when that last car just fell apart in front of his eyes. There were some missing elements in that car—obviously, some crucial screws were loose or missing (along with the engine and most of the other parts hidden behind the facade of the car body).

The movie turned out well in the end, but in real life a *missing element* often means the difference between excellence and mediocrity, success and failure, or even life and death. If the family is a foundational building block of God's kingdom, then we can't afford to overlook the missing elements in our families.

Something *is* missing in the kingdom. The King has inspected His kingdom and found us lacking the two most basic elements needed for success. I've already given away the punch line, so I'll repeat it again: The missing elements in the kingdom of God are real kingdom men and real kingdom women.

WE NEED KINGDOM MEN AND KINGDOM WOMEN IN KINGDOM ORDER

We have plenty of males and females running around, but it seems they don't know who they are, who God intended them to be, and how they are to work together in God's order and harmony. What we need are *kingdom men* and *kingdom women* united and cooperating in *kingdom order.*

These are just a few of the sad side effects of confusion and ignorance of God's purposes in the human race:

> For since the creation of the world His invisible attributes are clearly seen, being understood by the things that are made, even His eternal power and Godhead, so that they are without excuse, because, *although they knew God, they did not glorify Him as God*, nor were thankful, but became futile in their thoughts, and their foolish hearts were darkened. Professing to be wise, they became fools . . .
>
> Therefore God also gave them up to uncleanness, in the lusts of their hearts, to dishonor their bodies among themselves, who *exchanged the truth of God for the lie, and worshiped and served the creature rather than the Creator*, who is blessed forever. Amen. For this reason God gave them up to vile passions. For even their women exchanged the natural use for what is against nature. Likewise also the men, leaving the natural use of the woman, burned in their lust for one another, men with men committing what is shameful, and receiving in themselves the penalty of their error which was due. (Rom. 1:20–22, 24–27, emphasis mine)

CONFUSED IN THE VACUUM OF HUMAN WISDOM

When you don't know and understand God's plan for man, there is no way you can figure out how to be a real man or woman. The vacuum of misunderstanding and limited human wisdom may even skew an individual's direction-finding ability so badly that he becomes confused about which role is his.

It is amazing to see the void that comes in the absence of leadership. I remember watching a television documentary about the day former President Ronald Reagan was shot by a gunman. I still remember watching the actual news footage of the shooting being replayed at the time. Most of us thought that the president's wounds were minor and that he was in no real danger.

We had no idea that chaos had seized the nation's halls of government in Washington, D.C. We know today that President Reagan's wounds were nearly fatal, and his life was hanging in the balance. When the nation's leader was incapacitated, everyone started questioning everyone else. Secretary of State Alexander Haig contributed to the confusion by announcing that he was assuming control of the country, bypassing the Vice President.

The same thing happens in churches, ministries, and homes whenever there is an absence of leadership. People find themselves seizing authority unlawfully or following counterfeit leaders and usurpers.

God said that when people ignore the clearly visible attributes of deity in creation and refuse to glorify Him as God and are unthankful, then their thinking becomes futile and their hearts grow dark. When they profess to be wiser than God (or claim godhood for themselves), they become fools on parade.

There is a serious downside to the profession of rebellion—God lets go. He releases us to drown in our own sinful appetites when we begin the fools' parade. If we are determined to call "up" down, He says, "Fine. Change all the arrows and modify the signs—but you'll still be under the force of gravity." If we in our grand wisdom decide right is wrong and wrong is right, He says, "Okay. I'll let go and give you up . . . enjoy your new king, but watch out for the horns."

In the spirit realm, the conspicuous absence of the genuine always creates a vacuum that will quickly be filled by the conspicuously counterfeit. If real kingdom men and women are absent from the church, the community, and the world, then there are countless counterfeit versions waiting to step in and claim the rights and privileges of the real thing while providing none of the benefits or virtues provided by the genuine articles.

Overloaded with Preachers, Short on Teaching Priests

Another crucial problem plaguing Israel in King Asa's day (and the church in our day) is that they had lost their "teaching priests." In my opinion, we are overloaded with preachers and have a dire shortage of teaching priests. Preachers can build a four-hour shouting meeting out of half a word out of context mixed with some hot steam and some fancy preaching and performing techniques. Some of them remind me more of hirelings than of shepherds because they fly in on a wing and a prayer, preach up a storm without any substance, and blow out on the breeze with pockets lined with the wool of the sheep.

Real preachers are more like the "teaching priests" of King Asa's day. I don't care whether they shout it, whisper it, or deliver it with a lisp or a stomp of the foot—as long as they preach the uncompromised Word of God and stand behind it with their lives.

It is easy to win over a crowd with an ear-tickling, flesh-blessing message, but what happens when you lay down the Word of God and look folk in the eye? Are you prepared to say, "Thus saith the Lord . . .," even when the people in the house don't like what you've got to say? Where are the teaching priests who have the courage to speak the truth in love and march to God's beat even if it costs them their popularity and their big offerings?

I settled the issue long ago: I have not been called to be popular. God did not call, consecrate, and commission me as a pastor of sheep just so I could get along with everybody. I've been called to lead God's people to the place He has ordained. If I see the sheep in my charge going the wrong direction, woe be it unto me to keep my mouth shut and watch them take a fatal fall.

FORGET ENLIGHTENMENT—WE WANT ENTERTAINMENT!

No, I am determined to do everything I can to help those under my pastoral care follow in the footsteps of the Great Shepherd. We've come too far to get off the track.

But too many in America's churches refuse to hear or obey the instruction of a "teaching priest." Perhaps this explains why so many church congregations have moved from wanting enlightenment to craving entertainment.

Why are so many members of the body of Christ confused in their understanding of God's basic plan for life? They have no biblical concept of the true roles of men and women in the family and in the church. Notice that I said *biblical* understanding. We have plenty of half-baked theories, experimental concepts, personal agendas, and individual ideas, but no one seems to be asking God about it all.

Millions of people sit in padded church pews, wooden benches, upholstered seats, and even converted outdoor movie theaters every weekend, but most of them don't really want to be taught. They come to be reassured and entertained. No wonder so many church leaders feel the need to compete with Showtime, HBO, and wide-screen movie releases. (The reassurance is considered to be an automatic benefit of showing up—cleanliness and church attendance are next to, or perhaps equivalent to, godliness, according to their skewed thinking.)

The last critical missing ingredient plaguing the Israel of King Asa's day was that they had no law. When a culture adopts and promotes a false view of God based on bad information, God begins to remove His restraints of kingdom order, and evil begins to spiral out of control. That is what has happened in the United States.

GOD LIFTED HIS ORDER, AND LAWLESSNESS FILLED THE VOID

Since we have a skewed image of God based upon false information, God has lifted His order from our schools, courts, and legislative institutions. Lawlessness (the politically correct term would be *freedom of individual expression*) filled the void in less than a decade, and now we are a nation without vision and without restraint.

The book of Proverbs tells us, "Where there is no revelation, the people cast off restraint; but happy is he who keeps the law" (29:18).

Our nation is missing *God's rule* today. Sleazy television talk shows are a dime a dozen because there are no rules. There is such an appetite for fleshly thrills, outrageous acts of public rebellion, and feel-good experiences that TV and radio network programmers run anything-goes talk shows 24/7 on stations throughout America.

The only rule governing personal behavior for popular society in this nation seems to be, "What do I feel like doing?" Nobody has vision (unless it concerns personal gain or satisfaction), and so many people live without any self-restraint that Americans are rarely shocked by anything they see in public or in the media.

What happened? God lifted His rule. It is as if God watched us pursue every personal want and whim—everything except Him—and finally lifted His hands and said, "Have at it."

HELL IS GOD LIFTING HIS HAND

Do you want to know what hell is like? *Hell is God lifting His hand.* We are getting a sample of hell here on earth because we insist on going our own way without the rule and law of God. He is saying, "Have at it. Do you want sex? Have at it. You want to lust until sexual desire has lost all of its ability to please? Have at it. Do you want to make a total mess out of your life and destiny in the name of personal freedom? Have at it."

We cannot have order and structure in society without God. The problem is that we are not convinced. This is the land of the "self-made man," the bootstrap nation of self-starters with self-determination. No wonder we have no "true and living God." Despite our self-confidence and our ability to ignore our near-total disintegration from the inside out, the truth is that there will never be order and structure in America as long as America denies God.

So what happens to us when we don't have God? Most Americans avoid asking this question because they already suspect the answer. Those who do ask the question have their own answer ready: "We're free. Who needs Him—if He exists at all?"

Everybody wants to be free. We want to be free to breed like dogs (and kill our kids in the womb or abandon them in scattered locations around the globe). We want to do whatever we want to do, when we want to do it, the way we choose, as often as we choose, with whomever we choose—oh, yes, and we want to be free of any consequences.

The problem is that nothing is free in this world. The law of cause and effect is eternal and universal. *Somebody* always has to pay—if not you, then somebody else. The chief architect of the "freedom without consequences" rap also happens to be your most rabid and heartless enemy. When you become free on his terms, he makes sure that you become enslaved to the very thing you wanted in the first place.

Freedom enslaves the people of God because freedom without the order of God causes us to do things that are against our natural wills and against the rule of God. In reality, this kind of pseudofreedom apart from the grace of God actually kills us instead of bringing life.

REBELLION PROPELLED US OUT
FROM UNDER GOD'S ORDER

What is happening to our society? What is happening to life today? What is happening to America? It begins when we cry out, "We are free! We left the 'plantation' and the rule of man." Unfortunately, our rebellion and determination to supply our wants at any price also propelled us out from under the covering of God's order and blessings. Now we are out in the woods of willfulness doing whatever we want with no thought to the eternal consequences of our actions.

Too many of us call ourselves Christians while we continue to rob and cheat one another. We lie to one another—face-to-face and behind the back—and we appear to be grossly dysfunctional in virtually every kind of relationship requiring trust, honesty, and transparency.

Do you know what really makes me angry? I hate talking to people whose motives and moral track record force me to figure out what they *really* mean behind their smokescreen of words. Most of the time they don't mean what they say—they are simply angling for a position of advantage, power, or protection from exposure. They claim to be kingdom people, but they're just weasels.

I'm looking for people who mean what they say and say what they mean. I long to fellowship with people whose words are indistinguishable from the lives they live day after day. If they say a thing, then it is true. If they don't like something you've done, they "speak the truth in love" instead of stabbing you in the back in their very next conversation with someone else.

STOP PLAYING GAMES: BE A MAN! BE A WOMAN!

It is refreshing to look into people's eyes and know that if
something appears black to them, then they will call it black. If
it appears blue, then they will tell you it is blue. If they don't like
me or dislike something I've done, at least they'll tell me to my
face. Brothers and sisters in Christ, it is time to stop playing
games. Be a man! Be a woman!

One of the most shocking facts revealed in 2 Chronicles 15 is
that God *Himself* was the cause of Israel's distress. Israel had
plenty of enemies, to be sure, and then there was always the
adversary waiting in the wings for his chance to steal, kill, and
destroy. Nevertheless, Israel's problems came from their heavenly
Father's loving correction. When Israel failed to seek and obey
Him, God simply abandoned them to the terrible consequences
of their actions. Heaven's favor disappeared, God's mercy was
nowhere to be found, and His grace was conspicuously absent
from every area of life. It was hell on earth.

WELCOME TO HELL ON EARTH

In that sense, God is also the cause of my congregation's distress, and He is the cause of the body of Christ's distress as well.
It is not the devil! The unsaved people of the world aren't our
problem. When we sin and refuse to repent or seek His face, we
find ourselves in spiritual bankruptcy and face-to-face with our
righteous God Himself! Welcome to hell on earth (with the worst
yet to come).

If we want to know how to get back into the protection and divine covering of God, then we must understand that if He is our problem, then He is also going to be our only solution.

If you have been living "without the true God, without a teaching priest, and without law," you can stop fighting with the devil; he isn't your problem. You've come face-to-face with the holiness of God, and He isn't about to change or bend to accommodate your addiction to disorder and life outside the kingdom. Get right or get left outside (Matt. 22:1–14).

Did you ever get angry with your father (if yours was present in your life)? I did, and years later my own son became angry with me too. In my case, I became so angry with my daddy one day that I told him I was going to leave home. I packed what little I had, but I made sure he could see me because the truth was that I really didn't want to go. My daddy said, "Get the —— out!" He granted me my request.

HEADED FOR THE DOOR IN THE HEAT OF ANGER

That was not freedom; it was destruction in motion. Nevertheless, that is what we do. One night my son became so angry with me that he decided to leave too. If I remember correctly, he didn't even bother to pack. He just headed for the door in the heat of anger.

"Where are you going?" I asked.

"Leaving."

"Going where?"

"Umph . . . [growl]."

Listen—if your child threatens to leave but he still conducts a conversation with you, you know he doesn't want to go.

I just looked at my son and said, "You're a fool. You don't have anywhere to go. It is two o'clock in the morning. Wait until daylight, then leave."

He reluctantly came back in the house, and he didn't leave the next morning either. My son knew in his heart that freedom from Daddy isn't good because Daddy sees things that he couldn't see. He didn't really want to leave home; he just wanted to express his anger and push against the boundaries a little. I didn't want him to leave either, but it was my job as a father to protect him from his own anger and youthful naïveté.

Let me lay another crucial foundation stone: Not only have men and women failed to meet the kingdom mandate of God because we actually don't have a true concept of God, but we have been without teaching priests. Or we refused to heed the teachers God gave us because we just didn't want to hear it. When you fail to have a "hearing ear," you doom yourself to life without law or kingdom order.

As a pastor and bishop, I can tell you from experience what happens when I confront people with something controversial from God's Word. (Do you know what *controversial* means? It is usually "something you don't want to deal with according to the Scriptures of God.")

THEY CHANGE MY IDENTITY IN THEIR MINDS

The moment certain people in my church realize I'm messing with a favored sin, indulgence, or prized presumption, they change my identity in their minds. Can you guess who I become? They lay aside every recognition of anointing or divine appointment and say, "Oh, he's just a man. Who does he think he is? Why is he saying that?"

As a leader and equipper in the body of Christ, I have an obligation to preach, teach, and model the Word of God, not my personal opinion. If my opinions do come up in a conversation or sermon, I clearly label them as such.

When ministers of the Word stick with God's Word, it puts the burden of proof and obedience on the hearer. If the people read the same words and see the identical confrontational message in God's Word, then they are faced with a divine dilemma. They have no right to get upset with me—*God* said it. It is God Himself calling them to account—all I am is a messenger.

When someone rejects the Word of God after it is preached without compromise or reservation, he is basically saying, "To hell with God!" Please warn me if you are going to say that—I want the opportunity to move to a safer location some distance away. Last time I looked, my Bible still said:

> Of how much worse punishment, do you suppose, will he be thought worthy who has trampled the Son of God underfoot, counted the blood of the covenant by which he was sanctified a common thing, and insulted the Spirit of grace? For we know Him who said, "Vengeance is Mine, I will repay," says the Lord. And again, "The LORD will judge His people." *It is a fearful thing to fall into the hands of the living God.* (Heb. 10:29–31, emphasis mine)

WE REDUCE DIVINE MANDATES
TO MERE HUMAN OPINION

We have a dangerous human tendency to reduce offensive divine mandates to mere human opinions in our minds. "I'm not going to follow him or listen to what he preaches because Eddie Long ain't no better than me. Now if he wants to bless me with a car, I'll call him preacher, pastor, and even bishop. He just better not think he can mess with me in certain areas. I've got to do my own business, and he just gets too nosy. That's between me and God."

Which God? Don't make me take you to the book of Acts and the apostles' confrontations with demons and unclean spirits! People who hear the Word of God and refuse to put it into action in their lives have a telltale problem—a problem that plagues the body of Christ today. James said:

> Be doers of the word, and not hearers only, deceiving yourselves. For if anyone is a hearer of the word and not a doer, he is like a man observing his natural face in a mirror; for he observes himself, goes away, and *immediately forgets what kind of man he was.* But he who looks into the perfect law of liberty and continues in it, and is not a forgetful hearer but *a doer of the work, this one will be blessed in what he does.* (James 1:22–25, emphasis mine)

I'm determined to help men and women in the kingdom of God know who they are. We can't afford to miss the move of

God in this hour. My King told me to pay the price to write this book, and I did not need another assignment just to have something to do.

We are talking about an ancient nation named Israel that was deteriorating because the people did not have a true God, they had no teaching priests, and they had no law or kingdom order in their lives. The children of Israel forgot who they were.

It's Time to Look in God's Looking Glass Again

I'm concerned that the children of the King have also forgotten who they are in the twenty-first century. We are a dysfunctional family of the spirit that has majored on the hearing of the Word instead of the *doing* of it. Now we are paying a terrible price. It's time to look in God's looking glass again and recover our true identities as men and women of the kingdom.

It seems that about every two thousand years God brings about a major spiritual transfer and economic shift of power and resources. It is almost as if He allows the unresponsive and rebellious elements of the human race to accumulate massive stores of wealth and power just before He steps in to make a major readjustment or "bank-account transfer" from the coffers of the unjust to the accounts of the just.

What happened when God sent Moses to deliver His covenant people from slavery to a new identity as a holy people? The first thing He did as the slaves walked away from their slavery was to make the Egyptian enslavers turn over their riches to the enslaved! Read the Book. The day the Israelites walked out of

Egypt, the Egyptians willingly handed over their silver and gold (Ex. 12:35–36)!

THE GREAT CELESTIAL TRANSFER OF POWER

When Jesus came about two thousand years later, He humbled Himself to be crucified, to die, to be buried in a borrowed tomb, and to be resurrected from the dead. In that single act of supreme obedience, the great inheritance of God was loosed among mankind: "Christ in you, the hope of glory," and we were seated with Him in high places (Col. 1:27; Eph. 2:4–6). All of the resources of heaven and the kingdom were opened up to us, and we are still learning how to tap all of the wealth we received in that great celestial transfer of power and authority.

What is happening now? Revelation 12 speaks of a "male Child," hidden of God. Look closely at three events described in this passage:

> *She bore a male Child who was to rule all nations* with a rod of iron. And her Child was *caught up to God* and His throne . . . And war broke out in heaven: Michael and his angels fought with the dragon; and the dragon and his angels fought, but they did not prevail, nor was a place found for them in heaven any longer. So the great dragon was cast out, *that serpent of old, called the Devil and Satan, who deceives the whole world; he was cast to the earth, and his angels were cast out* with him. Then I heard a loud voice saying in heaven, "Now salvation, and strength, and *the*

kingdom of our God, and the *power of His Christ* have come, for the accuser of our brethren, who accused them before our God day and night, has been cast down." (Rev. 12:5, 7–10, emphasis mine)

The "male Child" hidden by God was actually the church rising up in Christ. The woman in Revelation was giving birth to much more than Jesus Christ; she gave birth to the holy thing—the church and God's kingdom on earth—that Jesus Christ actually brought to pass through His obedience as the Son of God.

ANOTHER SHIFT OF SUPERNATURAL EMPOWERMENT IS COMING

What does that mean? It means we are in a time and season when another great shift of supernatural and economic empowerment is coming to the kingdom of God. It also means everything that is holy to the Lord will be especially targeted for destruction by the enemy.

When Moses was about to be born as the deliverer of the children of God, Pharaoh issued an edict to kill every male child among the Israelites. When the pharaoh of the next generation refused to obey the order and command of God, the death angel was released to kill every male in the land—whether human or domesticated animal. Only the blood of an innocent animal had the power to save and cover.

King Herod targeted the male children for destruction when he heard the rumor of the true King's birth. If we are in another season of economic empowerment when God is ready to move through this "male Child" called the church, then we should be quick to recognize that males will be the favorite targets of the devil. In every instance, God used anointed and courageous women to bear and protect the male seed. In Moses' day, He used Moses' mother and sister and the daughter of Pharaoh to preserve His deliverer. In Jesus' day, He used Mary to bear the divine seed and nurture Him until He reached maturity.

We need the missing element in the kingdom as never before. We must discover our true identities and roles as kingdom men and kingdom women. We can't go through this alone, separated, or in the destructive track of spiritual ignorance. We must rediscover God's order for each human element in the divine plan for His kingdom.

Chapter 5

MEN, WE'RE HIDING

There is a new sound in the garden of God. We hear the rumor of approaching footsteps that span the ages from Genesis to Revelation. God is walking this earth and searching once again for Adam. *Adam,* the ancient Hebrew term for a human being. We sense His presence in a new way today—God has come in the time of habitation. He has come to take up residence with us—if He can *find* us.

Every time God draws near, a shaking comes to our lives as well. We have prayed for God to come; we have asked Him to spend time with us and to dwell with us in a tangible way. Now God is saying, "I am not visiting you. I've come to take up permanent residence in My kingdom."

That means it's time for a housecleaning. It means every kingdom man must stand for inspection according to unbending kingdom standards. The things we used to do won't do any longer. The King is preparing us for permanent occupation and divine habitation. Everything that can be shaken is shaking, and everything that can be shaken loose is being removed in the passage from visitation to habitation. Slow down and ask yourself these questions:

1. When I get to where I'm going, where will I be?
2. When I get to where I'm going, will I want to be there?
3. When I get what I've been wanting, what will I have?
4. Is what I want worth Christ dying for?

Don't get upset; get holy. It is all for our blessing and betterment. Some things never seem to change—especially on those days when God makes a personal house call to His kids in the vineyard:

> They heard the sound of the LORD God walking in the garden in the cool of the day, and Adam and his wife hid themselves from the presence of the LORD God among the trees of the garden. Then the LORD God called to Adam and said to him, "Where are you?" So he said, "I heard Your voice in the garden, and *I was afraid* because I was naked; and I hid myself." (Gen. 3:8–10, emphasis mine)

When things fell apart the first time in the Garden, God came to visit, and He specifically called for His chief gardener and ruler on earth. Yes, Eve had her part to play, and she had her sins to confess, but God called for Adam first because he was *responsible*.

HE STILL HOLDS MEN RESPONSIBLE

When it comes to straightening out the mess we're in today in this nation, God is once again calling on the sons of Adam. He calls for the men first because He *still* holds us personally responsible for every mistake made "on our watch." He also holds us responsible to follow through and make the corrective actions we are destined to make.

The only reason God's order and structure are messed up today is the sons of Adam are out of place. Jesus Christ finished His work on the cross, but we have just begun ours. Our nation is at risk because we're out of place. Adam's spiritual and positional dislocation produced something we still haven't shaken because we have refused to take up our crosses daily and follow the King (Luke 9:23).

It amazes me how we hide when we hear the voice of God. I've learned a lot while working with young men over the years. I'm open as a student to learn from those who regard me as their teacher and mentor. At this moment, I am pouring myself into a group of fifteen young men and teaching them about the stock market as well as laying a foundation of God in their lives.

At the same time, I am investigating their lives to learn what kind of baggage they carry from yesterday. What must be removed and what must be added to their lives to ensure their success? The amazing thing about it is that these young men are submitted to me. I have their attention, and they are willing to grow in the things of God.

Too many of us are unwilling to seek out older or more experienced people in the kingdom of God to help us break out of our bondages. If you are battling a spirit of poverty from your cultural or family background, it doesn't make sense for you to hang around broke people to help you break the chain of poverty. You should seek out men or women who are wise stewards of their finances, people who know how to make money and make that money work for them.

If you are single, you may want to fellowship with other singles who share your situation. However, if you really want to prepare yourself for marriage, you should seek out godly married people who will prepare you for success in marriage, and who may well introduce you to others seeking a mate. I realize this seems to be opposed to the usual view in the church, but so be it.

Somebody's hiding behind the bushes. Somebody's struggling to hide a whole body of nakedness behind the thin veneer of a fig leaf, and it isn't working. God is calling and somebody's still hiding—but not everybody.

At this writing, seven hundred men have been rising at five o'clock in the morning to join together in intense prayer every Tuesday and Friday. Many of them are urging me to add another day of prayer each week—not because they want to be with me, but because they hear the voice of God alerting them that something is about to happen.

These men from the Atlanta area, and millions of kingdom men like them around the world, are determined to prepare themselves for the task. They intend to be all that God has ordained them to be and to walk in their rightful roles as godly men in a holy kingdom.

Adam told God on the day of visitation, "I heard Your voice in the garden, and *I was afraid.*"

HIDING BEHIND THE BUSHES OF LIFE

Once again God is calling to the men hiding behind the bushes of life, "Adam, where are you?" and we're still saying, "I heard Your voice calling, and I was afraid. I hid myself because I was naked."

Men, we're hiding.

Why are so many fractured families and households struggling to survive in our culture and being supported and maintained by a single female provider? A man (if you can call him that) had to be there at least once for those children to get there.

We're hiding from responsibility because we're afraid. There is only one way to turn this around: "Somebody's gotta be a man." Someone must have the courage to stand up and make his life count. Someone must make his voice heard above the chaotic crowd. Someone must be willing to take the lead and take all the criticism his detractors can lay down. Someone, a man, must be willing to be thrown down for what he believes in.

Somebody, God's kingdom man, must follow in the footsteps of the Greatest Man and willingly lay down his life to save others. God is calling, but too many men are still hiding in the bushes of fear and withered manhood. "I'm too busy following the pennant race . . . I can't miss the football game, Lord."

Regardless of what many women believe, most men are fearful. The tougher they appear, the more fear they are hiding behind their macho fig leaves. They're afraid to let you see who they really are because, in their insecurity, they think that's only for "sissies."

God doesn't buy it either. He is waiting for men to come to their senses and openly confess, "I don't know everything, and I never did. To tell the truth, I don't even know what I'm supposed to be doing. I just want to walk through this and just get there."

GOD CAN STRIP YOU DOWN TO THE REAL YOU

Adam confessed that he was afraid when he heard God's voice in the Garden because he was naked. God is the only One who can strip you down to the real you. We can play identity games with each other, but if we spend time with God, He will quickly show us who we really are underneath all of the facades.

If you are a man and the fig leaves from your hiding place are still in your hand, God wants you to face your weaknesses and give them to Him. It's time to come out of the bushes and take over like a kingdom man.

When you wake up in the morning, confess your weakness to Him so He will make you strong. When I pray in the morning, there are certain things I'll tell God because I recognize who I am.

"Now, God, if this was presented, or if this was presented to me this way, I don't know whether I could resist it. I'm putting my weakness on Your altar, Lord. I need Your help in these areas." I get it all under the blood!

HE TRANSFORMS YOUR WEAKNESSES INTO STRENGTH

God wants us to acknowledge our weaknesses before Him because it puts the Holy Spirit in charge of those areas. He possesses the power to transform your weaknesses into strength. God told Paul, "My grace is sufficient for you, for My strength is made perfect in weakness" (2 Cor. 12:9).

Relationships are born out of vulnerability, including our relationships with God. It takes vulnerability and trust to share your inner thoughts and feelings with others. When men dare to share the inner heart with other brothers, they must *cover* each other. We don't run down the street and tell somebody else. We don't sell the story to the highest bidder on the sleaze talk-show circuit.

Too many men in the church are hiding. They are afraid to step out and take a risk to do something. Why? For the same reason Adam hid himself in the Garden. He was unable to accept the responsibility God gave him.

What did Adam do? He told God in his own words, "God, I'm mad at *You*, and I'm mad at *her*. *You* gave that woman to me, and *she* messed up."

God didn't buy Adam's excuses then, and He isn't buying ours today. He basically said, "Look, Adam, I don't care what she did. It doesn't matter what your children will do in the future. I don't care about all of that—I'm coming to you because *you* are responsible."

I submit to you that most men are still hiding behind the fig leaves of guilt today, and they're pointing their fingers at everyone except themselves. They are either mad at God or mad at a woman. Since they refuse to accept responsibility for where they are and what they've done, they claim their problem is with God or with some woman. All ignorance aside, *nothing will change until you accept responsibility.*

If you are in the same place you were three years ago, the only person you should blame is yourself. Don't blame somebody else because you are broke or hurt. Yes, it may be true that somebody hurt you or treated you wrongly. But the ball is in your court now. Do you want to be free? Do you want to go up instead of down?

Whom Do You Blame?

Stop pointing your finger, and step out for a new beginning. As long as you keep your finger pointing at others, you will never do what it takes to accept responsibility for a turnaround. As long as you have somebody to blame, you will never move to a better place and a better life. Whom do you blame? (That goes for *everybody*—for men *and* for women.)

Whenever my daddy saw men who wouldn't accept responsibility, he used to tell me, "They're slack."

I would say, "What do you mean, Daddy?" and he would reply, "They're slack. There's no weight to 'em."

Too many American men are lightweights masquerading as heavies on the stage of life. We drag our macho around like we're God's gift to women, but in reality a man without responsibility resembles a cancerous growth or a stray dog more than a gift from God.

The author of a book titled *Straight Talk to Men* presents a strong case demonstrating that irresponsible single men are actually a threat to society. He says, "Until they accept the responsibility for families, their sexual aggression is largely unbridled and potentially destructive."[1] He continues:

Men commit over 90 percent of the major crimes of violence. Men commit 100 percent of the rapes and 95 percent of the burglaries. Men comprise 94 percent of our drunken drivers. Men comprise 70 percent of suicides. Men comprise 91 percent of offenders against family and children. Single men comprise between 80 and 90 percent of most of the categories of social pathology and on the average they make less money than any other group in society, less than single women or working women. Eighty to ninety percent of all offenses are by single men.[2]

No Vision, No Responsibility, No Standards

Most single men seem to have no vision because they have no responsibility for a family or children. Many of them—in the world *and* in the church—spend their money and their weekends running to the clubs and singles bars in the pursuit of women, conquest, and the satisfaction of their sexual aggression.

They get drunk, they get high, they drive while under the influence, and *nothing* holds them to a higher standard. Many of them slip into the bondage of pornography and illicit drug use, and they constantly try to impress others instead of discovering their true identity and becoming a living and walking model.

Ticking Time Bombs and Wolves Among Sheep

When a man's aggression rules his existence, he becomes a ticking time bomb, a wolf among sheep. I can tell you what is missing. Carefully read this passage from Mark's gospel:

It came to pass in those days that Jesus came from Nazareth of Galilee, and was baptized by John in the Jordan. And immediately, coming up from the water, He saw the heavens parting and the Spirit descending upon Him like a dove. Then a voice came from heaven, *"You are My beloved Son, in whom I am well pleased."* (1:9–11, emphasis mine)

If you are a man, would you answer these questions? When did you become a man? When was your manhood affirmed? God spoke to my heart and said that many males act like children because they did not have a distinct time in their lives when they were called a man. Therefore, they refuse to take responsibility because they still think they are being judged as a child. One day while I was at Bishop T. D. Jakes's home, his son Dexter said something to me and then paused and said, "That was deep." What I just said to you on this page was deep. Now back up and read this page again!

Manhood has nothing to do with age. When did we put away childish things? Men, did we stop playing, or did we just change toys?

The problem with us (I'm speaking as a man about men in general) is our refusal to be responsible for where we are in life and for the people God places there. How much weight could be lifted from the shoulders of single mothers, widows, and the fatherless if the men of God would say this to themselves and follow through with their lives?

I've got to put away my toys. I feel the burden of their pain, and even though that is not my child and she is not my wife, I have a responsibility to tend to their needs. I am a kingdom man called to care for God's garden and the treasures He has planted there.

MY PAST WAS AFFECTING MY PRESENT

If you are a man, I challenge you to study your life. Go back into your past, and examine your patterns of perception and behavior. I had to deal with my past one time because something there was affecting my life in the present.

To my surprise, I discovered I was still operating as I did when I was seven years old. I still had temper tantrums and became angry when I didn't get my way. It wasn't pleasant, but I had to admit that I was still selfish at times. Worst of all, I realized I was still Mama's boy, and I expected my wife to treat me like that at times.

I still have to deal with these old patterns from time to time. However, once I recognized my problem, took responsibility for my actions, repented, and gave them all to God, He broke their grip on my life. They lost their power to dictate or contaminate my future.

Some of us have recognized the problems plaguing our lives, but too many of us are trying to affirm ourselves in the sandbox of life according to the traditions and wisdom of the world. It doesn't work that way because the Original Equipment Manufacturer didn't design us that way.

THE ANNOUNCEMENT THE UNIVERSE WAS WAITING FOR

What should we do? We should do things the way God does them. Notice that God the Father dealt with His Son, Jesus Christ.

When Jesus humbled Himself to be baptized by John the Baptist in the river Jordan (even though He had committed no sin worthy of repentance), God made an announcement. It was the announcement the entire universe was waiting for: "Then a voice came from heaven, 'You are My beloved Son, in whom I am well pleased'" (Mark 1:11).

The heavenly Father made this announcement declaring His approval *before* Jesus performed any miracles. This was *before* Jesus did any of His *Messiah* stuff. In the Jewish tradition, a *coming out* announces, "You are a man now. You have every right and responsibility of manhood."

When do human males become *men*? Our churches are filled with males of many ages who are still hiding behind their stuff. They may be twenty-nine, thirty-five, forty-three, or eighty-seven, but they are still blaming their failures, shortcomings, and nonachievements on everybody else. Meanwhile, God is calling out, "Adam, where are you?"

Many of the same statements could be made for females and their entrance into womanhood. In the natural, a female experiences a more dramatic physical transition at puberty than a male does. Her first experience with menstruation is a significant "coming of age" event, yet a young woman also needs a pronouncement, a formal statement from a father declaring his pleasure and unconditional approval.

ROOTED IN THE FATHER'S AFFIRMATION

Have you accepted responsibility for what God has *billed* to you? Once you say yes, He is for you and not against you. Being a kingdom person has nothing to do with what you are about to do—it is rooted in the Father's affirmation that even if you make a mistake, mess up, fall down, or totally miss it, you are still His child, and He is well pleased with you.

Too many of us go through life trying to prove things instead of resting in this great gift from our Father in heaven: "Even if I don't do anything right, even if I don't reach the end zone, my Daddy is still well pleased. He isn't committed to me based on my performance. He loves me just because of who I am. That means *I* can love myself because of who I am."

According to Luke's gospel, Jesus put His toys down at the age of twelve:

> When [Joseph and Mary] did not find Him, they returned to Jerusalem, seeking Him. Now so it was that after three days they found Him in the temple, sitting in the midst of the teachers, both listening to them and asking them questions. And all who heard Him were astonished at His understanding and answers. So when they saw Him, they were amazed; and His mother said to Him, "Son, why have You done this to us? Look, Your father and I have sought You anxiously." And He said to them, "Why did you seek Me? Did you not know that *I must be about My Father's business?*" (2:45–49, emphasis mine)

At first I'm sure the priests couldn't understand why Jesus preferred to stay in the temple while all the rest of the boys were outside playing. After the first question-and-answer session, they no longer wondered.

Twelve Years Old and
Teaching the Teachers

When Jesus' parents showed up three days later, they were so upset that they failed to notice how odd it was to see Israel's foremost religious scholars asking their twelve-year-old questions about the Scriptures.

All that Mary and Joseph wanted to know was, "Why are You here? We've been looking for You." He said something very significant, something that was tied directly to the beginning of His manhood: "Why did you seek Me? Did you not know that I must be about My Father's business?" (Luke 2:49).

God expects every male to rise up from spiritual infancy and become a kingdom man, fully absorbed in the Father's business. Most of the young men I talk to don't know anything about the Father's business. Their eyes are on the world and the flesh, not on the eternal kingdom. They are easily distracted and pulled away because they are not seeking the presence of God.

"You are My beloved Son, in whom I am well pleased" (Mark 1:11). What would happen if you asked every male you know, "When did you become a man? When did you become prophet, priest, and king in your home? When did you walk with the authority to prophesy and call people into their destiny? When did you learn how to fall on your knees and cover more than just yourself in prayer? When did you learn how to walk in such kingly authority and kingdom order that you brought order to every situation you're in?" That would be the day you received your Father's blessing and were released into manhood.

Too Many Males "Bail" When Things Get Tough

Unfortunately, most men would have to say, "I don't know what you're talking about . . . do you know when the football game starts?" What is the problem? Too many males "bail" or run when things get tough. They melt and run at the first sign of the heat of responsibility. Too few of them know how to persevere, and they are too easily offended and too slow or timid to speak the truth "in love" (Eph. 4:15).

Men, stop hiding. If a problem appears between you and another man, just ask him, "What's up?" Deal with him like a man, and look him in the face. Stop playing the world's back-stabbing, backward-communication game. Rise up and be a man, which means taking responsibility for your actions and reactions.

If a man in your church won't speak to you or appears to be offended, don't wait for things to "work out." Go directly to the man and say, "Is there a problem between us? This friction can't go on. It's time to uncover the problem and deal with it. You are better than this, and I'm going to speak to you every day until you open up and talk with me face-to-face."

If you are a man in the kingdom, you must understand that many of the problems plaguing women in the church are directly related to men in their lives who don't know how to love.

Every man in God's kingdom should memorize this passage from Paul's letter to the Corinthians: "When I was a child, I spoke as a child, I understood as a child, I thought as a child; but *when I became a man,* I put away childish things" (1 Cor. 13:11, emphasis mine). He said that right after he penned the most accurate and anointed description of love the human race has ever known.

SHE JUST FELL APART—BECAUSE DADDY DID IT

Do you know who can hurt a little girl more than anyone else? Her daddy can. Whenever I raised my voice at my daughter, she just fell apart. It was as if someone had killed her—because her daddy did it.

It doesn't seem fair. My wife could raise her voice at our daughter, but she never seemed to fall apart or react to it in the same way. Yet all I had to do was to say her name in a slightly stern tone, and she would collapse to the floor in tears. Was she being rebellious? No, she was expressing her hurt and dismay.

A daughter naturally desires the love and approval of the mature man who is her father. Anything that appears to be rejection, disfavor, or separation from that love sends shock waves through her heart.

God requires kingdom men to be responsible and put away childish things. Why? The greatest power a man possesses is a manly love that comes from God. It contains the unique ability to spark maturity in a boy and launch him into manhood.

This manly or fatherly love (I am not talking about a sexual love) that a man receives from God can envelop a little girl in a kind of unconditional love and security that begins her rapid transformation from being a little girl to becoming a mature woman.

THE LOVE THAT CAN TOUCH A GENERATION

The same love, when extended unconditionally from a husband, will ignite divine callings in his wife and help bring her into her own destiny. This fatherlike love even possesses the power to touch an entire generation and raise it up in God's purposes.

According to the Bible, you overcome evil with good (Rom. 12:21). Men who lay down their toys and rise up in Christ do not rape women, nor do they raise sons who mistreat and abuse women or children. Godly men do not inflict pain on those they are commanded to protect and honor, nor will they allow other men to harm them.

As men, we are responsible for all the pain we see around us. It is our job to fix what is broken, protect what is threatened, correct what is wrong, rebuke what is in error, confront what is out of order, and heal those who are wounded. We are responsible. The buck stops here at the feet of kingdom men.

We complain about the younger generation worshiping the so-called role models on MTV and BET, and in Hollywood's big-screen scandals. Yet we won't rise up and provide a positive, Christ-based alternative.

We'll shout at the devil from our easy chairs, but no one is willing to run to the battle for the next generation. Even a lion with no teeth can win a battle against a man with no backbone. We can't show them anything better because we are too preoccupied with our toys to back up our sass with brass.

Enough is enough. I'm studying God's Word. My mind is made up. I'm going to be something or die trying. I'm out to obtain the prize and capture the gold. I'm sick of meeting young men in the African-American culture who think the only way out of their urban hell is through rap! Who has fed them that lie? They are getting it from the bold "role models" standing in front of a Bentley luxury automobile they don't even own.

LAUNCHED INTO THE CULTURE LIKE AN ARROW

It's strange, but when a preacher gets a Bentley, people get mad. That's why I have two of them. God has launched me into my culture like an arrow, and I'll go to almost any lengths to plant the kingdom in their "hoods."

Long before those young men ever darken the door of a church, they need a visual sermon, a public declaration right on their street that shouts, "You don't have to be ashamed to be a man of God!"

I have those vehicles because I walk in integrity. They are the side benefits of saying yes to God. I can look in any man's eyes and say I haven't stolen anything, and I can sleep at night without a care in my head about God's judgment. (By the way, I'm not worried about jealous church folk either—the ones who don't understand God's mandate for kingdom men to stand up and take over in Jesus' name.)

While I'm on this soapbox, let me say that money isn't evil. It is the *love of money* that is evil. If David could have it and Solomon could have it, who said you can't? Who said it is off-limits to me? My job is to say yes to God; I can't help accepting the blessings He sends to overtake me along the way.

God has called me to be more than a preacher. He has called me to extend His kingdom into the business realm as well. So I'm a business owner. I am a priest and a king. Why? I am trying to stand and dare to take the land so other men can see Goliath fall and can take courage.

THE KINGDOM ANOINTING IS MORE
POWERFUL THAN ANY NATURAL GIFT

When they ask, "How do you get it done?" I point to God and His kingdom. I don't want them to think I accomplished anything in my humanness. I want them to see that kingdom men walk in a kingdom anointing that is greater and more powerful than any natural gift or ability they may possess. It is God who is at work in me.

Now we have come to a point of decision. If you are a man, do you recall a definite moment in your life when you *knew* you were called into manhood? If the answer is yes, then I challenge you to get to work and fulfill your calling in the kingdom. If the answer is no, then I must ask, "Are you ready to experience your moment *now?*"

If you don't have a definite moment in your life when you knew you were called into manhood, then you may find yourself responding to difficult situations in the same way you responded as a child. Don't be offended; I know how it feels. I was right there until God intervened. Now He has anointed me to intervene on your behalf.

Do you find yourself running from responsibility instead of taking a stand and doing what God ordained you to do? Do you catch yourself covering your backside with statements such as, "It's his fault," "Don't blame me; it's her fault," "The government did me wrong," or "My family ruined me when I was a kid, and now I don't have a chance"?

It does not make a difference who was wrong. What matters is where *you* stand right now. Too many innocent people are getting killed and hurt because people insist on discussing fault and fixing the blame. It is time to drop the accusing finger and extend the healing hand of a kingdom man.

Marking the Passage into Manhood and Responsibility

Let me say this the way I feel it: "We're fixing to have a bar mitzvah!" This is a formal ceremony observed by many Jewish families to mark the passage of a boy into manhood. *Bar mitzvah* literally means "son of the law," and it is a sign to the young man and his religious community that he has attained the age of "religious duty and responsibility."[3]

If you don't have a definite moment marking your passage into manhood, then you are about to get one. I'm going to pronounce your manhood, and I want you to understand that from this day on, you are responsible to operate as a kingdom man in every situation that comes your way.

Prayer and proclamations in the Spirit have no time or space limitations. In the book of Acts, we are told people were literally healed when they came into contact with handkerchiefs and aprons that had touched Paul's body (Acts 19:12). You and I can agree on this point right now as you touch these pages. Since it is an agreement in the Spirit, then it is binding in the eyes of God, no matter where you and I are at the moment.

First, you may need to clean out some junk hanging around in your "garage." If your marriage is nearly broken and your home is out of order, it is time to take responsibility. The next time you see your wife, be prepared to tell her, "It isn't your fault. I have decided to take a stand and accept the responsibility for what is wrong in our marriage. That means I also accept the responsibility to do whatever it takes to fix what is broken and correct what is wrong."

It Takes a Real Man, Not a Boy or an Older Male Pretender

Second, make sure you understand *why* you must step into kingdom manhood. It isn't because you need to impress other men or make more money on the job. When you begin to walk in your position as a kingdom man, God will release that manly love through you that we discussed earlier. This kind of love has nothing to do with sexuality, but it has everything to do with God's power to heal, restore, and establish order in the earth. The hitch is that it can be released only through a real man, not a boy or an older male pretender.

Since God has called me to be a transparent preacher, I often reveal a lot of things about my relationship with my earthly father. He was like any other man in the sense that he had his weaknesses and he made his share of mistakes. However, I can tell you one thing about my father that made a lifelong impact on me as a boy: He was a *man*.

When my daddy walked in the house, order came in the door with him. I could not sleep until my daddy's key hit the door.

My mother loved and nurtured me, and I was Mama's little boy in many ways. But I could never really rest until Daddy entered the house. He was a real man, and he walked with a real man's authority. When he came in the house, I knew there was no demon in hell or on the earth that could bother or harass me. I literally felt that secure whenever Daddy walked in the house.

The Holy Spirit seemed to drop a thought in my spirit as I thought about these things, and I realized that certain men and women would read these words who are still suffering from feelings of abandonment and betrayal.

Perhaps there was a time in your life when you needed your daddy and he wasn't there, and you've never really recovered from that point of failure. Only God knows how many foolish decisions and fractured experiences grew out of the void when your daddy wasn't there when you needed him.

WHEN I NEEDED HIM THE MOST, HE WASN'T THERE

Perhaps you wanted him to tell you that he loved you, but he never told you that. I can remember the moment when I needed my daddy the most, and he was not there. God gently reached into my heart and touched the point of my pain. This is your moment; this is your appointment for healing. Pray this prayer with me:

Father, forgive him, for he didn't really know what he was doing or why. Help me to forgive him too. I release my father from every failure, fault, and foolish act he ever did. I even forgive the unforgivable because You forgave me. Heal the wounds in my heart, and restore the joy of Your salvation, Lord. In Your power and grace, I accept responsibility for a fresh start free from the hurts and wounds of the past. In Jesus' name. Amen.

Now just before we have our bar mitzvah, I have to ask if you have a problem apologizing to others. Is it difficult for you to look into the face of your wife or of another man? Are you able to admit that you offended someone and honestly say, "I'm sorry"? Kingdom men accept responsibility for their sins, offenses, and mistakes.

When we complete this pronouncement over your life, you will discover that you have a new grace and ability to acknowledge your mistakes and apologize to others.

Now I want you to move to a private place where you can close the door, avoid interruptions, and concentrate on the work of God in your heart without distraction.

Just a Catalyst in a Spiritual Transaction

This is a spiritual transaction between you and God—I am just a catalyst. The Holy Spirit is the One who is about to do a supernatural work in your heart and life. Lift one hand to the Lord, and read the next few passages aloud so you can hear them. At God's direction, I stand in the place of your earthly father with the command to make this announcement of affirmation from your heavenly Father:

> *You are My beloved son in whom I am well pleased. I know your weaknesses. I know about your public failures and your secret sins. I know where you've been, and I even know where you were last night. I know all there is to know about you, but because you seek Me with all of your heart, I want you to know that I am still pleased with you.*
>
> *I know your vices and I know your fears, but I also know what you are capable of doing. And I am still pleased.*
>
> *Now, at this very moment, I want you to turn over to Me every failure, weakness, sin, and fear in your life. You have come of age in the Spirit; you have stepped forward before Me to take responsibility for where you are and who you have become. Now I am released to turn your life around. To the degree that you release these things to Me, I will remove their power to hurt, enslave, and contaminate your life and the lives of those you love. Remember, nothing is impossible for Me.*

Today I declare that you have become a man—fully equipped, fully responsible, fully knowledgeable, fully yielded to the Holy Spirit. Every curse that has been placed on you I declare has been destroyed in the name of Jesus Christ.

I declare that you are called to sexual purity for the rest of your life in the name of Jesus. I declare that divine prosperity has been released in your life, divine healing is released in your body, and God has given you a right spirit and a clean mind.

Now it is your turn. Make this declaration before the Lord, and do it out loud.

TODAY I AM A MAN!

I am a man, and I am responsible for the created order of God.

I take full responsibility for the condition of those You place under my care and authority from this day on.

I will cover everyone You place in my life.

Healing shall flow from me to their bodies.

Uplifting words and deeds will flow into their lives and hearts from the gift You placed in me as a kingdom man.

I will respect and honor my wife as the precious queen of my life; and I will respect every child under my care as a child of the King and the inheritance of God. I accept responsibility as a man of God, as a man of Your kingdom, and as a man given charge to tend, care for, and protect Your kingdom treasures.

· *Chapter 6* ·

WOMEN: LIFE GIVERS AND WALKING EPISTLES

O ne of the greatest gifts God gives to us when we enter His kingdom is the ability to discover who we are. Every fresh separation from God's original touch, beginning with the sins of Adam and Eve in the Garden, weakens our links to our true identities as the sons and daughters of God. Sin severed the connection, but Jesus Christ the Vine came and died to reconnect us to God through Himself.

The most significant "reconnections" include the reconnection of kingdom women to the calling of the first kingdom mother, Eve. She was the first human female, and God personally crafted her from elements taken directly from Adam's side. She was specifically designed to be Adam's helper and coregent on the earth. Even her name bears eternal kingdom significance, although Adam named his wife after their fall from innocence: "Adam called his wife's name Eve, because she was *the mother of all living*" (Gen. 3:20, emphasis mine).

According to *Strong's,* Eve's original Hebrew name, *Chavvah,* means "life-giver." The root of that means "to live, to declare or to show."[1] Just as Adam said Eve was "the mother of all living," I sense that God is declaring to every godly woman today, "My kingdom women are *life givers.* You are the 'mothers of all living.'" Man carries only the seed; it is the woman who bears the womb, nurtures the seed, and brings forth life in due season.

DID YOU MISS THE POSITIVE PROPHECY IN THE MIDST OF THE CURSE?

This brings up another crucial truth about women that many in the church go to great lengths to ignore. Many people think that the confrontation between God and the first couple ended purely in a curse, but they are overlooking one of the most significant and most positive prophecies in all of Scripture.

Look closely at this exchange between God, Adam, Eve, and Satan in the book of Genesis:

> The LORD God said to the *serpent:*
> "Because you have done this,
> You are cursed more than all cattle,
> And more than every beast of the field;
> On your belly you shall go,
> And you shall eat dust
> All the days of your life.
> *And I will put enmity*
> *Between you and the woman,*

And between your seed and her Seed;
He shall bruise your head,
And you shall bruise His heel."

To the *woman* He said:
"I will greatly *multiply your sorrow and*
    your conception;
In pain you shall bring forth children;
Your *desire* shall be for your husband,
And he shall *rule* over you."

Then to *Adam* He said, "Because you have heeded
the voice of your wife, and have eaten from the tree of
which I commanded you, saying, 'You shall not eat of it':
"Cursed is the ground for your sake;
In toil you shall eat of it
All the days of your life.
Both thorns and thistles it shall bring forth for you,
And you shall eat the herb of the field.
In the sweat of your face you shall eat bread
Till you return to the ground,
For out of it you were taken;
For dust you are,
And *to dust you shall return."* (3:14–19, emphasis mine)

Satan (who was already cursed with banishment from heaven)
received yet another prophetic curse with God's prophecy that
"the seed of the woman" (speaking prophetically of the birth
of Jesus from Mary's seed, but not Joseph's) would crush his
head.

Eve was cursed with multiplied sorrows (part of life in a fallen, sin-ridden world), pain in childbirth, and a shift in order. Suddenly, the rule of law entered the relationship between Adam and Eve.

Adam's sin brought a curse to the earth itself, and it doomed him to lifelong struggle for survival. Worst of all, the last five words declare that Adam (in this case meaning all of mankind) was placed under the curse of physical death.

THREE CURSES WITH A BLESSING

The third chapter of Genesis records three curses with a divine blessing hidden in the middle. God said, "I will put *enmity* [hostility and hatred] between *you* [Satan in the form of a serpent] and *the woman,* and between your seed and her Seed; He shall bruise your head, and you shall bruise His heel" (Gen. 3:15, emphasis mine). From that day forward, there has been mutual and undying hostility between women and the spiritual snake we call Satan.

Do you want to know why so many mamas have successfully pulled their children from the flames of hell after spending decades on their knees in unyielding prevailing prayer? It is because God has anointed them with a fighting spirit when it comes to protecting their seed from Satan.

In virtually every culture, every fool knows you don't step between a mama and her children. That is a good way to lose a limb or altogether end your life early! Don't mess with a mama. She'll go right through you, even if you do outsize her by a hundred pounds and eighteen inches.

Woman of God, your Creator gave you that fighting spirit for a holy reason. He equipped you to carry on unceasing war with Satan and his seed-stealing crew. It is probably safe to say that Satan really doesn't like women. Every time he turns around, a kingdom woman is giving birth to another deliverer right under his fire-singed nose, so he hates everything about you.

He especially hates getting caught by a kingdom mother when he's trying to steal her seed—all hell breaks out over his head in those moments because God anointed the woman with a mother's passion and a holy fury to deal with him in a fight.

Men carry a heavier weight of ruling authority in them, and they are born for the battle. But they also have a problem. Most of the time, men take too long to get mad at the devil.

A Kingdom Mama Runs for Her Holy Spirit Rake

A kingdom woman gets mad at that snake every time she smells him. She sees red every time she even thinks about somebody trying to touch her children, and a holy fury rises up in her. At the very first sign of the devil, a kingdom mama is running for her Holy Spirit rake. She instinctively grabs her Hoe of Faith and goes for that pointy head.

A man wants to check everything out and make sure it's a snake before he does anything. His child could be long gone before he would ever get around to putting on his snake-stomping boots.

I share a problem that plagues a lot of married men: Sometimes I find it difficult to admit that my wife is right. The truth is that my wife has such a wonderful discerning spirit that

I sometimes refer to her as "Gladys Kravitz" (the "nosy" neighbor in the old television series *Bewitched*). She isn't nosy, but she is constantly on the lookout for unusual activity in the spirit realm and in human behavior.

Her ability to sense abnormality in details is especially acute when it comes to her own children in the home. I will never forget the time my son tried to start his own "sneaker factory-reconditioning" business. He discovered that if he sent his basketball sneakers back to a particular shoe manufacturer, their policy was to respond to any complaint about defects by sending the customer a brand-new pair.

MY WIFE STAYED ON THE CASE

Packages were going back and forth from our house, and my wife discerned there was something wrong. She urged me to investigate, and my son told me he had just sent in his defective sneakers for a replacement. I told him, "Just go ahead then," but my wife stayed on the case (and on my back).

Finally, I went to Kodi and said, "Look, you have to help me with this. I'm tired of your mama coming to me about all of these packages." He admitted he had told some of his school friends about the generous sneaker-replacement policy and promised them he could trade their old shoes for new ones. We immediately put a stop to his emerging shoe racket, but it was only because my wife had such discernment and a "fighting spirit" to match. She sensed that the devil was trying to ensnare our son in a secret sin involving illegality.

How do we reap the benefit of *both* strengths in the home and in the church? I heard of a kingdom man who sat around in the garden while the devil seduced his wife—and that man acted as if he didn't even know that snake was there (see Gen. 3:1–6 for the whole sorry story). God's solution is to join a man's strategy, strength, and authority with a woman's life-giving nurture, extra sensitivity, and holy fury toward unholy things that creep and steal.

God knew what He was doing when He gave women this extra sensitivity to the archenemy of the human seed. It is the woman who carries a child from conception to birth nine months later.

In the kingdom, women are the mothers of all life. Women are the anointed nurturers while men don't seem to know how to nurture or nurse anything (unless it is some kind of wound or ache that might win some soothing sympathy from Mama).

A Woman Is Far More Attuned to the Task of Nurturing

A man can plant a tree, but *she* will have to water it. I can bring my wife seed, but she will have to labor to bring it forth in birth. It is the woman who nurses a child at her breast and holds a little one close for the first three years of life. She is far more sensitive because she is far more attuned to the task of *nurturing new life*.

As I noted earlier, this fighting spirit in a woman is most effective when linked together with the authority and power of a godly man and husband. He tempers her passion with the deadly calculation and skill of a warrior. Together, God's passionate life giver and God's fierce protecting warrior can decimate the enemy's ranks.

We know what can happen when a man and a woman work together in God's kingdom, but what happens when a woman finds herself married to a man who does not know God or understand the kingdom?

The apostle Peter provided the answer and revealed another amazing gift God gave to women: "Wives, likewise, be submissive to your own husbands, that even if some do not obey the word, they, *without a word, may be won* by the conduct of their wives" (1 Peter 3:1, emphasis mine).

SUBMISSION WAS UNIVERSALLY UNDERSTOOD TWO HUNDRED YEARS AGO

Somehow we've allowed the word *submissive* to become a nasty word over the last two centuries. Until the emergence of representative democracies or republics in France and the United States two hundred years ago, submission was universally understood around the world. Why? Until that time, virtually every nation on earth was ruled by a king or by some other version of a monarchy.

Monarchies are rare today, and we have muddied the waters of understanding with Western terminology. Contrary to uninformed opinion, biblical submissiveness has nothing to do with narrow concepts of subservience. In other words, God never said women were created to be "barefoot and pregnant."

The biblical concept of submission does not imply that women are airheads, intellectual lightweights, or inferior to men. If anything, it implies the opposite. It takes greatness to submit to authority when you know you are as capable as the one wielding the authority.

We are expected to submit to a police officer whether we are brain surgeons, CEOs of blue-chip corporations, the governors of states, or Navy SEALs on shore leave. It doesn't matter that the officer may not have attended college or doesn't own his own house. We respect what he represents.

Sorry, Sir: It Takes a Womb to Carry a Baby

Men and women are equal in essence and value before God, but they do not have the same functions in the kingdom. No matter how much a man wants it, prays for it, strains and grunts, or begs God for it, he will never conceive a child and carry it to full term in his womb. Why not? Isn't he just as good as a woman? He is just as good, but God did not give him a womb.

In the same way, God never intended for a woman to function as a man. Both genders were created to function and prosper in the places unique to their own calling.

What about a woman who is to be submitted to a husband who does not know God? Should she demand that he get saved? Should she fast and pray in her locked bedroom until he repents? Maybe she should refuse to serve him until he agrees to go to church or nag him until he turns from his wicked ways.

No, all of these things have been tried, and they all have failed. God has a better idea, and He spoke through Peter to give women a prophetic tip and a great deal of hope. He was saying (according to the Eddie Long commentary):

Listen, daughter. You don't have to beat the man with your Bible. You don't have to yell at him, fuss at him, or deprive him of your love either.

Use the secret weapons I gave you at your new birth. Show him your inner power and an inner beauty.

If you are willing to tap into who you really are in Me, if you will dare to tap into your divine femininity, you can save your husband's soul without so much as quoting a Scripture.

I have given you the power to become *a walking epistle* of My love.

Is "Walking Epistle" a Job Title?

Who would ever believe someone could save a man without quoting a Scripture? I think it is time for *us* to believe God's Word. He said they may be won "without a word." Believe His promise, woman of God. You've just been given a new job title: walking epistle.

If a kingdom woman does what it takes to walk in her true calling, she will become a walking epistle. When a man looks at her, he will say to himself, "I know that's the truth." A kingdom woman possesses the power to bring godly conviction to a man without saying anything. You can house the Holy Spirit like nobody else, and when you walk into people's lives or step into a situation clothed in a submissive spirit before God, people will just have to respect you.

"Where do you get all of that, Eddie?"

What happens when a uniformed member of the U.S. Marine

Corps or of the local police force enters a room? The uniform actually symbolizes two things at once.

First, it symbolizes *submission*. The U.S. Marine is submitted to the authority of superior officers in the U.S. Marine Corps, and to the authority of the United States government. The police officer is submitted to the community issuing the law enforcement officer's commission to carry a gun and enforce its laws.

Second, the uniform symbolizes the *authority* proceeding from submission.

Any kingdom woman who dwells with her unsaved husband dressed in the uniform of a submissive spirit before God also exercises great authority. She doesn't have to raise her voice to make her point.

God Will Raise Him

A godly wife doesn't need to nag, threaten, beg, or whimper. All she has to be is the lady God called her to be. Believe me, that husband will take notice.

What about the millions of Christian women married to saved but barely functioning husbands? We're talking about the Christian husbands who can spout every sport statistic reported since the first Olympic Games in Greece, but who can't even tell you where John 3:16 can be found.

In church after church, the majority of women attending services are fairly well versed in God's Word while their husbands aren't. If you want your man to become a man of the Word and a working citizen of the kingdom, then strut your stuff. Allow the Holy Spirit to shout life into that man through your loving ways and godly lifestyle.

I know that sounds good, but it also sounds real religious, and that isn't good enough. Now for some very practical advice. (Let me warn you in advance that this is for married couples. I don't want unmarried cohabiting couples—that's the politically correct term for *fornicators*—telling people that Bishop Eddie L. Long told them to "get busy" like they were married people. I didn't and you shouldn't. Repent, get right, get married, or separate.)

There Is Something You Can Do

If you want your husband to come to church and he won't, or if you want him to let *you* go to church and he won't, there is something you can do: Draw your husband into the kingdom with love and unmerited grace. After a while, curiosity will prod him to go to church with you just to find out what suddenly made you treat him like a king. God doesn't force us to love Him, so we shouldn't try to force our mates to love Him either. Do it God's way. Draw your husband into the kingdom with intimacy and grace. Fix him his favorite food. Do whatever it takes. Play with his toes or rub his bald head; just do *something*.

Perhaps you are thinking, *What do you know about it, Bishop? You are a man, a successful man in a high position.*

I've tried to share the Word throughout this book, and where I've injected opinion, it was based on the Word and years of experience working with thousands of situations involving marriage relationships. Yet you *do* have a point.

My "First Lady's" opinion matters the most to me, but I've also learned to appreciate the wisdom of other wise women in the kingdom. For that reason, I've included the testimony and ministry of Pastor Darlene Bishop in this chapter. She is a kingdom woman, a wise woman, a wife, a mother, a *young* grandmother, and a respected minister of the Word:[2]

> I got married when I was seventeen (and I'm still married four decades later). I married the most spiritual man in the church (he was really just a nineteen-year-old boy) who played the electric guitar and sang. When my husband would get up and sing, all of the young girls in that church would go right across the platform at altar call.
>
> I already knew I was called to the ministry, so I thought at the time, *I'll marry this guy, he'll be a preacher, and I'll be a preacher's wife. That's what God has for me.*
>
> Little did I know that right after I married him, the man would become so involved in business that he would quit going to church! (He went maybe once a month.) My solution to the problem was to nag at him. I'd say, "You're going to hell. Did you know that you're going to hell?"
>
> My husband was a millionaire by the time he turned thirty, and that was when a million dollars was a million dollars. As for me, I had come from nothing. I didn't even know you were supposed to put meat on sandwiches until after I was married. (All I had growing up were mayonnaise and sugar sandwiches and two dresses to my name.)

I hounded my businessman husband every chance I got. "Are you going to church Sunday? Well, I don't guess you are. You'll probably *plan* something so you won't have to go."

THE MORE I INTIMIDATED, THE FARTHER HE MOVED AWAY

I was trying to make him into something he didn't want to be, and I was trying to intimidate him into doing something he didn't want to do. The more I intimidated him, the farther he moved away from God. Finally, he started staying away from home just to escape the hounding. He only came home about two days a week just to change his suitcase and take me to bed.

I had four children during this time. I was so miserable that I actually prayed, "God, I've got to get this man out of my life." I spent my time spending money but it only made things worse. Finally things reached the desperation stage and I prayed, "God, You've got to help me. I've got to do something. I'll teach Sunday school, I'll work in the nursery, I'll do whatever there is, but I've *got* to get help. I've got everything any woman would want, but I need a husband. I need somebody to help me. God help me!"

I QUIT FUSSING AND STARTED FEEDING HIM

Then I heard the Lord speak to me, "Get into the Word." I dove into the Word until it became my life. Within six months, I quit fussing at my husband. Every time he'd come in, I'd be in the Word of God or I'd be studying the Word, and I'd say, "Honey, can I get you something to eat?" And I never said *anything* about God. I never said *anything* about going to church because I was too into my Father.

I was satisfied now because I had a *real Man*. I had the Man that the woman at the well had an encounter with. I didn't worry about any other thing.

Within six months God literally knocked my husband off of his horse, turned him around, and within a year from that time, we opened our first church with twenty people.

. . . it takes a wise woman. When you neglect your husband in some area there will always be a Bathsheba *bathing* so he can see her. There will always be a Delilah inviting him to lay his head in her lap.

And honey, I can assure you, Delilah isn't saying, "Take out the garbage! Do we have money for rent? Hey, the kids need to pick up. Clean up the garage." Oh no. That woman is getting busy running bathwater and lighting candles. She constantly whispers in his ear, "If *I* had a man like *you,* I'd take care of him."

MARRIAGE IS A MINISTRY

If you are thinking, *What is she talking about this for? This isn't ministry!* You are mistaken. Marriage is a *ministry.* God has anointed you to take care of your spouse's need, whatever it is.

At the first opportunity, you need to look at your companion and say, "I'm anointed for you." Ladies, you need to understand that women can get things done that men can't get done. Esther saved a nation by cooking a dinner. She won a nation by being submissive to the king. She didn't just march in there and say, "Listen to me, man!" No, she prepared herself in advance, and then she submitted to his authority and entreated him as his bride.

Marriages are being challenged today as never before. Our challenge is to love one another with our imperfections. If you are living with an ungodly mate, don't leave him. The Bible says your submissive and chaste life will save him. As long as you stay in the house, God's got a way to get to him.

If you are a woman, my prayer for you is that you have discovered or reaffirmed your identity in Christ as a life giver and a walking epistle of God. If you are a man, I pray that your eyes have been opened even more to the mystery and wonder of a godly woman in God's hand.

May none of us get through this encounter with God's Word *unchanged*. If you are single and committed to the kingdom life, you are about to have an encounter of your own in the following chapter as we discuss the dangers of "dating the devil."

Chapter 7

DATING THE DEVIL

S ome of the most frustrated people on the planet may be sitting next to you in church. You will find them singing in the choir, faithfully teaching Sunday school every weekend, or leading an outreach to some inner-city area.

Are they Christians? Yes. Are they filled with the Holy Spirit? Yes. Are they tithers and students of God's Word? Most of them. How, then, could they be "some of the most frustrated people on the planet"?

They've been dating the devil. Some of them even pledged vows of fidelity and marriage to him!

Now that I have your interest, let me ask you what you know about "yokes." Do you know what a yoke is? A yoke joins together two draft animals such as oxen or horses to maximize their pulling power. Yokes were also used to humiliate and control prisoners or defeated foes. The "steering wheel" for many aircraft is also called a yoke. It is something that ties together or links one thing to another.

You will have problems if you hook up with a man or woman who does not know who he or she is in Christ. You don't want to be linked with someone who does not spend time with the Lord or doesn't know the Word of God.

Sister, if you linked up with him because "he's just cool, he's got a cool rap, a car, a house, and all that" (and he doesn't have a submitted relationship to Jesus Christ), then he just might wrap you so tight in hell that you will not know how to get out of it! Marriage can be the closest thing to heaven or hell on this earth.

Mister, if you linked up with that woman just because she looks hot and acts hotter, then she might lead you down the hot road to hell as well. You don't follow Christ with your hormones; you love and serve Him with everything you've got! You begin by offering Him your body as "a living sacrifice, holy, acceptable to God, which is your reasonable service" (Rom. 12:1).

MARRIAGE TAPS INTO THE SPIRITUAL DYNAMIC OF UNITY

If you hook up with somebody who doesn't know the kingdom, you may feel as if you are the most frustrated person in the world. God planted an eternal destiny in your life, but your destiny is also tied up in the person with whom you share that life. He designed us that way to tap into the spiritual dynamic of unity unique to the marriage covenant.

This is the "yoke of love" between two people in which "the sum of their whole is greater than the sum of their parts." One plus one in this kingdom covenant doesn't equal two; it equals three—God Himself makes up the third element of power. This cannot and does not happen when one of the partners fails to understand the kingdom and its covenants.

What does a "yoke" have to do with Christians and "dating the devil"? The apostle Paul used the word when he warned Christians in the church at Corinth:

> *Do not be unequally yoked together with unbelievers.* For what fellowship has righteousness with lawlessness? And what communion has light with darkness? And what accord has Christ with Belial? Or what part has a believer with an unbeliever? And what agreement has the temple of God with idols? For you are the temple of the living God. As God has said:
>
> "I will dwell in them
> And walk among them.
> I will be their God,
> And they shall be My people."
> Therefore
> "Come out from among them
> And be separate, says the Lord.
> Do not touch what is unclean,
> And I will receive you.
> I will be a Father to you,
> And you shall be My sons and daughters,
> Says the LORD Almighty." (2 Cor. 6:14–18,
>   emphasis mine)

ANOTHER NIGHT AT THE MEAT MARKET

The problem is that most kingdom people think they can sample and choose companions and mates the same way the world does. All we do is "go to the meat market" and gauge the value of the hunk by its color, size, shape, and overall look.

Kingdom people don't belong in or on the devil's meat market. This sexual soul trap is one of his most effective tools for destroying human lives and inflicting misery on the human race.

What is the answer? Amos the prophet said it in a very simple way:

> Seek good and not evil,
> That you may live;
> So the LORD God of hosts will be with you,
> As you have spoken. (Amos 5:14)

Do what the King says, and you will prosper. Do what you want regardless of what He says, and you will reap what you sow without God's help or protection.

When you do what He says, you are putting practical feet to your spiritual commitment. At that point, you are no longer carrying the load by yourself. Jesus said, "Take *My yoke* upon you and learn from Me, for I am gentle and lowly in heart, and you will find rest for your souls. For *My yoke is easy* and *My burden is light*" (Matt. 11:29–30, emphasis mine).

What burden is He talking about? The original Greek word translated as "burden" means "an invoice (as part of freight), i.e., (fig.) a task or service:—burden; something carried, i.e., the cargo of a ship:—lading."[1]

LIVING "IN YOKE" WITH JESUS

The burden of Christ includes the kingdom destiny He planted in us long before we were ever born. He shoulders the real weight of the future, so our goal should be to do what we see Him doing and say what we hear Him saying. He set the example for us by only doing and speaking the things He received from His Father (John 5:19–20; 8:28). This is a real picture of living "in yoke" with Jesus.

Kingdom men are in great danger if they hook up with women who are not part of the kingdom and submitted to the same King. Just ask Solomon what happened to him. He went from being the wisest man in the world to becoming the most henpecked husband the world has ever known! Why do I dare to say such things about the great King Solomon? Because they are true.

God specifically warned this wise man against dating the devil by falling in love with and marrying "foreign women." He did all right for a while, but then he started dating the devil and wound up in bed with him—or at least with one thousand of his worshipers!

> King Solomon loved many foreign women, as well as the daughter of Pharaoh: women of the Moabites, Ammonites, Edomites, Sidonians, and Hittites—from the nations of whom the LORD had said to the children of Israel, *"You shall not intermarry with them*, nor they with

you. Surely they will turn away your hearts after their gods." Solomon clung to these in love. And he had *seven hundred wives, princesses, and three hundred concubines; and his wives turned away his heart.* For it was so, when Solomon was old, that his wives turned his heart after other gods; and his heart was not loyal to the LORD his God, as was the heart of his father David. For Solomon went after Ashtoreth the goddess of the Sidonians, and after Milcom the abomination of the Ammonites. Solomon did evil in the sight of the LORD, and did not fully follow the LORD, as did his father David. Then Solomon built a high place for Chemosh the abomination of Moab, on the hill that is east of Jerusalem, and for Molech the abomination of the people of Ammon. And *he did likewise for all his foreign wives,* who burned incense and sacrificed to their gods. (1 Kings 11:1–8, emphasis mine)

SOLOMON: THE MOST HENPECKED HUSBAND OF ALL TIME

Solomon ignored God's counsel and hooked up with one thousand foreign idol-worshiping wives, becoming the most henpecked husband of all time! When this wise man and majestic king gave in and helped his wives build altars of sacrifice to all of their idols, he relinquished his throne, forfeited his manhood, and sowed his own destruction and the doom of Israel.

The only acceptable sacrifice for some of those demon entities (particularly Molech and Chemosh) was the blood of innocent infants sacrificed in the fire. (What does this say about Christians and church congregations that have married the world and looked the other way and avoided any confrontation over the abomination of federally funded child sacrifice through abortion?)

Ask Samson why he had to settle for a second-best ending for his life as a blind and humiliated judge of Israel. He dated the devil and put his head in Delilah's lap. In the end, he lost his hair, his anointing, his sight, and his freedom (Judg. 14:1–4; 16:15–30).

Not too long ago, I had a preaching engagement that required me to leave on Sunday. In the past, I used to dress casually for travel and just mix in with the crowd. On this particular Sunday, I was feeling really good. I didn't have to preach that day, and I decided to dress up.

You will understand what happened if I tell you that when I looked into the mirror that day, I literally impressed myself. I was feeling good, and I told myself I was really *looking* good too. Another difference about this trip was that I had decided to travel alone. I usually take great precautions to avoid every appearance of evil. If I'm not traveling with my wife, I take along one of the men in my ministry. Not on this day.

SET UP FOR A DATE WITH DESTRUCTION

I didn't know it, but the devil was trying to set me up with a date for destruction. I walked through the airport telling myself, "Eddie, you really look good today." Then I noticed a striking young lady who was looking at me with obvious interest. She came up to me and struck up a conversation. Since I was feeling so good about myself in a fleshly way, I just decided to talk with her.

Later in the conversation, the young woman propositioned me. She said she wanted to meet and spend some time together. Now I *could* pretend I was unmoved, but the truth is that I wasn't always so "superspiritual." For a brief moment, her words flattered me. But then the Spirit of the Lord seized me and led me to think about the consequences of pursuing such a dangerous course.

I thought about my wife and how much I loved her. I considered how much it takes to build a marriage and a relationship based on trust. I thought about my children and how much they love me and look up to me. I thought about the congregation I pastor and how much they respect and trust me. I thought about the television audience I have and the influence I have in the city and what it really cost me to receive it. I thought about the tears and the pain my mother and father went through to put me through college and cover me.

I looked at the woman in that moment and said, "I'm too expensive. The moment that you want to spend with me would cost me too much." I turned her down and refused her advances. I walked away, rejoicing in the fact that God had brought me through a dangerous temptation. When I considered the great investment God and His people had placed in me, I knew I could not afford to even entertain the thought of dating the devil. It's true for your life too.

It is especially important for a kingdom woman to be yoked with a proven kingdom man. She is, in effect, choosing her earthly partner in the kingdom. It is especially difficult for kingdom women who marry outside the kingdom to fulfill their destinies and callings. The problem is, the spiritual heads in their homes do not serve the same King as they do. We have already discussed God's solutions in this situation, but they aren't easy.

Unequally Yoked and Tied to Another Soul

Many Christians don't seem to understand the importance or power of spiritual soul ties or "yokes." The Scriptures go into great detail on the subject, revealing the spiritual dynamic governing sexual liaisons in particular.

> Now the body is not for sexual immorality but for the Lord, and the Lord for the body. And God both raised up the Lord and will also raise us up by His power. Do you not know that your bodies are members of Christ? Shall I then take the members of Christ and make them members of a harlot? Certainly not! Or *do you not know that he who is joined to a harlot is one body with her?* For "the two," He says, "shall become one flesh." But he who is joined to the Lord is one spirit with Him. Flee sexual immorality. Every sin that a man does is outside the body, but *he who commits sexual immorality sins against his own body.* Or do you not know that your body is the temple of the Holy Spirit who is in you, whom you have from God, and you are not your own? For you were bought at a price; therefore glorify God in your body and in your spirit, which are God's. (1 Cor. 6:13–20, emphasis mine)

Let me just say that sexual union is far more important and far-reaching than most people will ever know. It creates powerful ties, links, or yokes between you and your partner's body, mind, will, emotions, and spirit (we will cover this in detail later in another chapter).

USING THE SAMUEL METHOD IN THE CHURCH SINGLES POOL?

Too many of us use the Samuel Method for choosing our mates—even though we think we're okay because we have restricted our shopping list to the lineup in the church singles pool.

Samuel was one of the great spiritual leaders and prophets of Israel, but when God sent him to select and anoint a replacement for Israel's King Saul, the prophet still fell for the temptation of choosing the best-looking candidate.

> Then [Samuel] consecrated Jesse and his sons, and invited them to the sacrifice. So it was, when they came, that he looked at Eliab and said, "Surely the LORD's anointed is before Him!" But the LORD said to Samuel, *"Do not look at his appearance or at his physical stature, because I have refused him. For the LORD does not see as man sees; for man looks at the outward appearance, but the LORD looks at the heart."* (1 Sam. 16:5–7, emphasis mine)

The Samuel Method shows up in the strangest places. We see it plastered on the sides of buses, in airports, in virtually every television commercial and magazine ad, in every political campaign imaginable (including the presidential race, unfortunately), and even in our church leadership appointments. We are all wrapped up with nothing inside.

NICE ON THE OUTSIDE, DEMONS ON THE INSIDE

We need to forget the standard of outward appearance. Handsome men and beautiful women are nice, but just ask yourself how many serial killers, women abusers, and despotic tyrants were actually very nice-looking in appearance, yet they harbored deadly demons within.

Don't trust your destiny and future happiness to a purely outward standard based on the distribution of a quarter inch of body fat and a fraction of an inch of human skin. Measure the person's depth with the rule of the Spirit of God. (That goes double when you are thinking about allegedly Christian candidates. Some people spend just enough time in church to run a really good scam and learn the Christianese lingo—especially men on the prowl.)

It only took one warning from God to get the prophet Samuel back on the God track. He wasn't going to repeat the mistake he made with Eliab, the eldest son:

> Jesse made seven of his sons pass before Samuel. And Samuel said to Jesse, *"The LORD has not chosen these."* And Samuel said to Jesse, "Are all the young men here?" Then he said, "There remains yet the youngest, and there he is, keeping the sheep." And Samuel said to Jesse, "Send and bring

him. For *we will not sit down till he comes here.*" So he sent and brought him in. Now he was ruddy, with bright eyes, and good-looking. And the LORD said, "Arise, anoint him; for this is the one!" (1 Sam. 16:10–12, emphasis mine)

DAVID DIDN'T HAVE THE POPULAR LOOK OF THE DAY

Since the Bible makes a point of describing David's appearance as "ruddy" (red-hued skin and hair), it probably wasn't the popular look in Israel at that time. David was a good-looking man, but it seems from Samuel's first choice that the Israelites preferred tall, dark, and handsome.

God had a higher and better standard—the standard of the heart. He wanted the prophet to choose the one man in Israel who was "heart qualified" for the job. This was the man of whom God said, "I have found David the son of Jesse, *a man after My own heart,* who will *do all My will"* (Acts 13:22, emphasis mine).

Remember two things: First, you will never find the best that God has for you by evaluating the outward appearance of a man or woman. Second, God's best is just that; it is the very best. He will bring you the right one if you let Him.

RUN THAT "FINE" PACKAGE THROUGH A SPIRITUAL X RAY!

I don't care how fine he or she may look; you need to take the wrapper off and check it out. Don't do it the world's way, though! I'm not talking about getting physically intimate with someone outside marriage. I'm talking about examining the contents of the package using a *spiritual* X ray. I'm talking about getting real and keeping it real.

"What are you saying, Bishop?"

Tap into the wisdom of God. Submit yourself to Him, to His Word, and to those in authority over you. Seek godly counsel, and take your request to God. Then "let go and let God."

When you place your heart's desire in His hands and submit to His wisdom, you release God to work on your behalf. He isn't about to let you down. If you insist on staying in control of the situation, then don't expect God to bless your mess. He won't do it.

Watch this now! You can attend every Promise Keepers Crusade, Women's Retreat, Ladies' Advance, or even "Woman Thou Art Loosed 50," but God will not work His supernatural will in your natural life as long as you hold back, hold on, and try to control your own destiny.

You won't land in His perfect will by trying to look at situations and circumstances and making your own judgments about what to do. The Scriptures declare,

> Trust in the LORD with all your heart,
> And lean not on your own understanding;
> In all your ways acknowledge Him,
> And He shall direct your paths. (Prov. 3:5–6)

If you follow this path of wisdom, you throw the burden of the relief on God in His sovereignty.

HAVE YOU WILLINGLY PUT YOURSELF UNDER LAWLESS DOMINATION?

On the other hand, when you date a non-Christian or even a non-kingdom person, you are subjecting yourself to all of that person's power and natural gifting—potentially under lawless domination.

Imagine for a moment what happens to a household or human spirit put under the influence of a servant of Satan. Do you realize that this is exactly what happens when you link yourself to a non-Christian person? No one can serve two masters (Luke 16:13). If the one you're with isn't serving Jesus in absolute obedience, then by default he's serving the adversary of your Lord and the enemy of your soul.

I've said it before and I'll say it again: We have things reversed. In the world, people date to marry. Kingdom people marry to date. Don't waste your money on an Internet dating service. There is no way it can measure the virtue of the human soul (or the lack thereof).

Commit your heart's desire (and your heartache) to the Lover of your soul, and *trust Him* to supply your need perfectly. There has never been a matchmaker like God. If your perfect match doesn't exist, then He has the power to create that one!

Which would you consider the true "class act"? To have your clothes custom made and custom tailored to your body, or to pull whatever you find off the crowded one-size-fits-all counter at the local discount store?

Forget Off-the-Rack Jack
and Beelzebub's Bootie Buffet

When you have God working on your behalf as your divine matchmaker, you don't need to go shopping for Off-the-Rack Jack at the devil's discount male-order store. You don't need to go sampling and nibbling around at Beelzebub's New-and-Used Bootie Buffet.

It is time to live like true kingdom men and women under the authority of the King. We must trust Him to personally select, prepare, and lead our mates and life partners to us. It all comes back to trust and faith.

When Eve emerged from the hands of God, she was focused on her Creator. She wasn't looking to Adam for her fulfillment; he was just the chief side benefit of her relationship with her Father in heaven.

My wife and I had the privilege of hosting a show for married people on TBN recently during which we talked with Dr. Fuchsia Pickett about marriage relationships. Sister Pickett brought out a wonderful point. She said that her husband "messed her up and made her mad" when he told her that *he could never make her happy.*

That comment posed a serious problem for her at the time for the same reason it would bother most young brides today: The precise reason she got married was to find fulfillment in her husband.

God Agreed with Her Husband!

Dr. Pickett said she went through years of fits because of what her husband had said. Finally, she went to the Lord only to discover that *God agreed with her husband!* He told her, "I am the only One who can make you happy. I am the only One who can fulfill you." I assure you that those words are just as true for men as they are for women.

Make God your first focus, your first love in life. Find your fulfillment in Him, not in other people, in activities, or in things. Jesus told the church at Ephesus:

> I know your works, your labor, your patience, and that you cannot bear those who are evil. And you have tested those who say they are apostles and are not, and have found them liars; and you have persevered and have patience, and have labored for My name's sake and have not become weary. *Nevertheless I have this against you, that you have left your first love.* Remember therefore from where you have fallen; *repent and do the first works,* or else I will come to you quickly and remove your lampstand from its place—unless you repent. (Rev. 2:2–5, emphasis mine)

Our marriages are becoming miscarriages because we marry one another hoping and trying to be fulfilled in flesh when God never intended for marriage to function that way. Fulfillment comes from Him; the blessings of the marriage covenant flow out of that inward fulfillment to each partner. If you entered marriage focused on extracting happiness or fulfillment from your spouse, you have misdirected and messed up God's order for your life.

YOUR NEW BEGINNING BEGINS WITH A CHOICE

Anything set up or operated outside of God's order can produce only chaos and "every evil fruit." Better said, you cannot break God's laws. They break you. The good news is that no matter how badly you began, God offers you a new beginning right now. And the beginning begins with a choice:

> *I repent and I choose Your way, God. Forgive me for my sin and my error. Guide me into Your divine order and the security of Your kingdom. In Jesus' name. Amen.*

The best way is to avoid becoming unequally yoked in the first place. That begins when you are still single. Avoid dating to marry if at all possible. Leave the matchmaking to God, and when you do marry, then marry to date.

You shouldn't feel that you've found Mr. Right or Miss Perfect unless the person passes the Holy Spirit X-ray exam.

Does this person *know who he or she is in Christ?* Does this person *know where he or she is going* and *why?* What is happening in the person's life as far as God is concerned? What do the seasoned men and women of God say who work closely with this person? Does this person exhibit the character of Christ and the kingdom during the week as well as on Sunday morning?

Above all, never, ever become so desperate for fulfillment that you just grab the first able-bodied person you see. Don't try to justify your desperation with religious catch phrases. I've seen desperate singles eyeing the altar at altar call, just hoping a good-looking man or a hot-looking young woman would come for salvation. "Oh, I like that. Look, girl, he's going to the altar. He just got saved! Now I'm going *after* that."

BEFORE HE EVEN STARTS SEEING THE LIKES OF YOU . . .

No way, sister. That boy needs to discover his new identity in Christ. He must know his responsibility under God to be a godly covering for you. He needs to learn and absorb God's Word. Above all, he must learn to draw his fulfillment from God before he ever starts seeing the likes of you!

"Well, I'm not married, and I'm tired of it."

Before I was married, God brought a lot of people into my life—people I was never meant to marry. Their assignment in Christ was to enhance my life and move me closer to completion in Him. Learn to take joy in the godly relationship God sends your way. Take time to smell the roses, and enjoy every beautiful moment God brings to you.

He will specifically send along members of the opposite sex who understand the kingdom. They will walk in relationship with you and receive something special from you, and they will also impart something special to you. Each of these God-sent relationships will help prepare you for a successful marriage relationship because they will teach you how to develop a lasting friendship to form a foundation for a lasting marriage.

Let me say this in particular to women in the kingdom: Be especially careful to maintain godly relationships with older mar-

ried men and their wives, and with those in the church who
extend pastoral care for you. This is for your protection.

God intends for men to know His Word. When Eve was talking to the snake, she heard some partial truths from him and
accepted them as fact without discerning the deceit and twisted
heresy in his intent.

WHAT'S YOUR DADDY'S NAME AGAIN?

Whenever a single woman talks to a man who does not know
the Word, that man may unintentionally take the place of the
snake in the Garden.

"How can you say that, Bishop?"

Any man who does not know God and submit to His Word does
not belong to God. That means that his spiritual daddy is Satan.

It is just as if the woman is talking to the devil. This is the reason: If that man cannot tell the woman undeniably and accu-
rately what God has said on a subject, then the words he does
speak may lead her against the will of God. The fruit of the conversation and the relationship are the same fruit produced by
Eve's conversation with Satan: deception, sin, and ultimately separation from God.

Don't mess with the devil. Don't look at the devil. Don't talk
with the devil. Above all, don't date the devil, or you might end
up in the marriage from hell.

If you run with a man outside the kingdom, then in the course
of your conversations and relationship he could miss just one
word, and you could change just one thing in your beliefs based

on his words that could curse you. You deserve better than just a saved man. You need a sanctified man. You deserve a mature kingdom man.

Whether you are a man or a woman, walk with someone who is walking with God or else you may discover you are dating the devil!

Now I have a word for single men in the kingdom: If you don't know God, if you don't know His Word, then you are not qualified to date. Do you want to know why? Those hot babes you are looking at with lustful eyes are actually precious daughters of God, the very apples of His eye. What do you think will happen to your soul if you mess up one of God's precious creations? (I'll let you answer that.)

Next we deal with the legal maximum-occupancy limit for your bedroom.

Chapter 8

HOW MANY PEOPLE
ARE IN YOUR BED?

The average church congregation, especially in an urban area, includes people from many walks of life and just as many spiritual levels of maturity. Many of the people born since World War II are suffering the effects of cultural revolutions that basically rejected behavior standards based on biblical morality and embraced sexual "experimentation."

This approval of sexual promiscuity is all that many young people have ever known—that and the specter of divorce that always seems to haunt those who practice it. The story is all too familiar. First you mess yourself up with this one for six months, then you break up and move on to the next sex partner.

After a rocky year and a half of sleeping with Dr. Jekyll and Mr. Hyde, you decide you've had enough sexual experimentation with the schizophrenic from hell. You make the break and decide to begin sampling the sexual hors d'oeuvres at the local singles bar, and you get into other unpleasant things.

What you don't know is that you are contaminating your spirit because you are becoming one with people who don't know who they are. They don't even know what to do with the physical "equipment" they were born with or why God designed it the way He did.

Worst of all, they don't know how they permanently damage a person's spirit with their indiscriminate sexual liaisons. They don't realize that STDs (sexually transmitted diseases), as bad as they are, comprise just the tip of the promiscuity iceberg. The truth is that people riding the promiscuity merry-go-round don't understand anything about themselves. All they can tell you is, "I've got this need for companionship."

When someone tells me this, I immediately agree and say, "Yes, you do! The One who created you also calls you to Himself because He wants to be your companion. He wants to be your lover and your keeper. He wants to tell you why He called you."

"Honey, Do You *Know* These People?"

Now it's time to bring up something you will probably never hear preached or discussed from a pulpit. It has to do with a problem plaguing many of the married people across our nation. What is the problem? A growing number of married people are discovering that when they make love, there are more than two people in the bed!

"What do you mean, Bishop?"

They are not alone because they dated around before their marriage, and they weren't pure.

Just about this time, most people in the typical church audience would secretly think to themselves, *What a prude! Come on, Bishop, break out of the fifties and catch up with the times! Nobody is pure anymore.*

Precisely. That is the problem.

My response to such critics is bold, cold, and blunt: Wake up, sinner! Come on, break out of your devilish slumber, and face the living God! Nobody is happy anymore because nobody is pure anymore!

God's kingdom order for sexual purity is never out of date. Countless civilizations, empires, dynasties, and philosophies have passed away, yet He is still securely seated on His throne.

I introduced this truth in the previous chapter, but now we must look at it again and probe for kingdom truths to heal our wounded souls and marriages:

> Do you not know that your bodies are members of Christ? Shall I then take the members of Christ and make them members of a harlot? Certainly not! Or *do you not know that he who is joined to a harlot is one body with her?* For "the two," He says, "shall become one flesh." But he who is joined to the Lord is one spirit with Him. Flee sexual immorality. Every sin that a man does is outside the body, but *he who commits sexual immorality sins against his own body.* Or do you not know that your body is the temple of the Holy Spirit who is in you, whom you have from God, and you are not your own? For you were bought at a price; therefore glorify God in your body and in your spirit, which are God's. (1 Cor. 6:15–20, emphasis mine)

WHO IS SHIRLEY?

What happens when a man and a woman have sex and then separate and continue their lives with other people? They may have disconnected physically, but in the spirit realm they are still one, just as a husband and wife are one. (This may help exasperated wives understand why their husbands are trying to get them to "do it like Shirley.")

The chances are high that there is a "Shirley" buried somewhere in the husband's spiritual memory container. He keeps comparing his wife's sexual performance with that of other women with whom he has been "one" in the past.

You have no idea how often Christian counselors, pastors, and church staff members hear Christian men and women confess with embarrassment, "I can't explain it all, but I just can't seem to shake these images in my mind. They always seem to come up at the worst possible moment."

HOW MANY PEOPLE HAVE YOU MARRIED?

If you are married, let me ask you a question: How many people have you married? Does the question irritate you? Did I hit too close to the mark?

Perhaps your problem is that you are married to too many people. I realize that there are still some people in the kingdom who did things God's way, so they can tell you the exact date and time of their first sexual encounter—on their wedding night.

Many other folks in the modern church, unfortunately, really want to forget the first (illicit) sexual encounter, but it sticks in their memories in full color. Every detail seems to be permanently outlined in their hearts, even though it took place, for some, decades ago. Why? They "married" that first sex partner on the level of the spirit.

When you have sex with someone, you take on an element of that person's spirit that never leaves you under normal conditions. So now you're carrying around Johnny or Latifah. As far as your memory goes, "There ain't nobody like Latifah." Like it or not, old Latifah still enjoys "joint-occupancy rights" with you as your spiritual wife.

You didn't realize it then, but you married that girl the moment you had sex with her. Now you are doomed to compare every sexual experience with that first encounter with old Latifah. The day came when you met Patricia and married her (but you didn't mention that Latifah was hanging out in the bedroom of your mind as well). Patricia gets tired of competing with the invisible lover who keeps showing up with you in bed, and she leaves you to search for somebody who does it like *her* first lover, Bob.

Finally, you meet and marry Shirley, the love of your life. At last, you know this one will work out . . . if she could just learn to do it like old Latifah. The only problem is that every time you and Shirley go to bed for a time of marital bliss, Latifah and Patricia show up too.

ONE NIGHT OF DELIGHT, A LIFETIME OF FRUSTRATION

This same problem also plagues millions of promiscuous singles today. They are constantly tormented by the spirits of all their one-night stands and spring-vacation flings.

It is bad enough when one partner battles the images of past lovers every time intimacy comes to the marriage bed. Things get out of hand even more quickly when *both* partners in a marriage must deal with the images of past intimate moments with other people.

Add to that mess all of the brokenness and emotional pain you can pick up over a lifetime of dealing with less-than-perfect people who intentionally and unintentionally hurt you.

Now take it a step farther. Even medical researchers will tell you that every time a person has sexual intercourse with a sexually promiscuous partner, he is actually having intercourse with *every person* that person has been with—and with every partner *those* people have had, and with all of *their* partners, and on and on.

This sad scenario has allowed such sexually transmitted diseases as the HIV/AIDS virus, gonorrhea, syphilis, genital herpes, and chlamydia to sweep through large segments of the population in Africa, Asia, and large cities in the United States and Europe.

OCCUPANCY: 2, MARITAL POPULATION: 152

Imagine the small town of spiritual soul mates populating the typical marriage bed of former "swingers" from the sexually liberated sixties. Now imagine what happens with their grandchildren when *they* get married! They consider the so-called sexual freedom pioneered by their grandparents to be a personal "right" and have multiplied their infidelity to an infinite degree (with the willing help of a sex-saturated media and entertainment industry).

The inevitable result is a version of spiritual "multiple-personality disorder" on a massive scale. I've noticed that many formerly sexually promiscuous people say they feel fractured and "thinned out," as if the personality has been parceled out to too many people through sexual liaisons.

Be prepared for World War III if one of the multiple-personality spouses accidentally begins to act like one of the partner's less-than-faithful lovers from the past. He doesn't know it, but his head is about to roll because she is ready to cut him off at the shoulders.

"You know you weren't at any gas station getting gas. It only takes five minutes to get gas, and you were gone a lot longer than any five minutes. Don't shake your head no; you were out there hookin' up with somebody at the hotel."

"Baby, I was only gone eight minutes. I know I'm quick, but come on now, I got driving time."

You Won't Find Mr. Right Passing Time in the Wrong Place

Do you want to avoid this nightmare in motion? Let this truth sink deeply into your heart: When God has somebody for you, He will lead you to that person or bring the person to you. You just won't find Mr. Right at the singles meat market. As for Miss Perfect, if she *is* perfect, then she certainly wouldn't waste her time in a social sex mill.

People who don't know who they are always seem to be searching for their identities through other people.

James the apostle seemed to describe the generation of the twenty-first century with prophetic accuracy in his short exhortation about the double-minded man:

If any of you lacks wisdom, let him ask of God, who gives to all liberally and without reproach, and it will be given to him. But let him ask in faith, with no doubting, for he who doubts is like a wave of the sea driven and tossed by the wind. For let not that man suppose that he will receive anything from the Lord; he is a double-minded man, unstable in all his ways. (James 1:5–8)

Many of us today just don't know who we are. We are all mixed up, messed up, trying to get hooked up with somebody else just because he looks good.

"Why do you like him?"

"Because he looks good."

Never Buy a Pig in a Poke

We need to reclaim an old saying from bygone days that says it all. The old-timers used to say, "Never buy a pig in a poke." Most people—even hard-core city people—know what a pig is, but very few of them know what a poke is.

"I just can't figure out who would want to poke a pig. Besides, what does pig abuse have to do with buying anything?"

Let me help with a little information from below the Mason-Dixon line. In the South, the word *poke* may also mean "bag" or "sack." The old saying was warning people against buying a pig in a bag where it was impossible to see it or inspect the animal for defects or disease.

If we are truthful, most of us must admit that we have been

hurt at one time or another because we picked out friends, went out on dates, or selected lovers based solely on their outer wrappings. We didn't take the time to verify what was on the inside before we bought the pig in a poke and brought it home.

I hope and pray that some of us, at least, are older and wiser today. When my son says, "I've got a friend," I'll say, "Tell me about this. Tell me about that." When he inevitably says, "I didn't ask her that," I'll say, "Why *didn't* you ask her that? Why aren't you finding out about this?"

Young men and young women (and some who aren't so young) often come up to me and say, "How do I know if I should be dating so-and-so?"

I'm going to share the answer I give them: If the person you are dating isn't good enough for you to marry right now, then you have no business dating that person. Why? Because you might mess up and discover you have begun the process of bringing a baby into the world. That means you either allow the baby to be born or consider murdering an innocent infant. (If you have had an abortion, don't condemn yourself. Pray the prayer of forgiveness right now. Now receive forgiveness and move on with your life. Your life is still very important to God.)

Now you have the grand opportunity of messing up the lives of *three* people. Unfortunately, person number three didn't have a choice in the matter, but inevitably, that person will pay the heaviest price for your foolishness.

If you are thinking seriously about marrying someone who is a kingdom person, you should ask, "Who have you been with? How many spirits do I have to deal with if we marry?"

I know this kind of talk goes against everything the popular sexuality of the world stands for, and I praise God for that! The world tells you that sexual love is your ultimate security. "I've gotta have somebody with me all the time. I've just *gotta* have me a man," you might say, or "I've *gotta* have me a woman."

What this really means is, "I don't know who I am!" Basically, the more you *gotta,* the more you *don't know* who you are.

More and more young people are marrying out of desperation today. There are vast numbers of young women and young girls who give their bodies to lustful and uncaring young men because there is no substance inside. They believe that the only thing they have to offer is their beauty and sexual favors.

MAMA DRESSES MORE PROVOCATIVELY THAN I DO!

If a guy threatens to leave them, they give up everything because they don't realize God made them to be queens. No wise woman ever told them who they are. Their only guide to femininity in life was watching Mama dress more provocatively than they do as she got ready for yet another wild night on the town.

If you are the single parent of a daughter, may I ask, when was the last time your daughter saw you really praying? When was the last time you looked into her eyes and gave her counsel filled with godly wisdom?

"Look, baby, I know the rest of the girls are dressing like that, but your hem is coming down. You're pretty. You're beautiful. It is okay for young men to notice your beauty, but you don't have to flaunt it.

"Major on your inward person; focus on the godly character God is molding in you. You don't have to run after every style and every 'do' at the hair salons. Understand that you are an original. If anything, you are to be copied. Know who you are, and don't settle for anything less than a king among men."

If you are a single man, you may not appreciate the way kingdom life "cramps your style," but there isn't much style in the way most single men run around like dogs in heat: "Gonna get me a woman."

Get Under the Influence, Not Under the Skirt

Unless you are under the influence of the Holy Spirit, you will probably feel the pressure to spend every free minute "chasing skirts." It is better to stop, repent, submit to the authority of the King, and discover who you are in Christ. If you don't, then you won't know how to handle a real woman. Despite your best efforts, you will mess her up before she even gets started.

God wants only the best for you, and God's best is *the* best. He wants you to enjoy a lifelong relationship of refreshing friendship, loyalty, love, and sexual satisfaction. He wants His married children to develop and enjoy a refreshing relationship in which both partners are giving, loving, yielding, and submitting to each other in an atmosphere of mutual respect. This will be difficult if you come to the marriage bed with clouded memories and sordid sexual histories.

I have good news for you if you are convinced "it is already too late." It isn't. God, in His mercy and wisdom, wants to give you a fresh start and a new beginning starting *now*. What is today's date? Write it down on a piece of paper, and plan to keep it as a sign and memorial to God's faithfulness.

DO YOU WANT JUST ONE MATE FOR A CHANGE?

This question may not apply to everyone who reads this book, but I have to ask you this question anyway: Are you ready to get rid of all the "other people" you married in the past? If so, you should know that a divine divorce is about to be decreed, and you will be left with just one mate and marriage partner for the rest of your life.

The memories of how Judy or Billy used to do it are going to leave you, and they will be replaced by a virginal purity covering your relationship with your spouse under God. The power of the prayer of agreement knows no boundaries of time or distance, so this is your chance to tap into the power of God and restore kingdom order to your life and your marriage. Put your hand on your heart, and pray this prayer with me:

> *Father, we thank You in the name of Jesus for Your great love and sovereign grace. Please forgive us of our sins and cleanse us of our unrighteousness.*
>
> *On this day I pronounce in the Spirit that the spirit of purity in this marriage is restored—whether it was lost or stolen through illicit sexual union, seduction, abuse, or rape. Purity and holiness in this marriage union are now restored in the mighty and wonderful name of Jesus the Christ.*

In Your name, I also declare a divorce of every unautho-
rized spouse and companion joined through the sin of sexual
promiscuity or violence. These spouses who are married under
Your authority and kingdom order are now married to one
another and one another only. We ask that You sovereignly
release and remove all other spirits from their hearts, bodies,
spirits, and memories. We thank You for it in Jesus' mighty
name.

I declare right now that you are a new man and a new
woman, healed, set free, and released unto your divine destiny
in the kingdom of God. Father God, I ask for a supernatural
healing for every woman who has been injured at the hands of
a man, be it through the sin of incest, rape, physical abuse,
verbal abuse, wrongful seduction by deceit, or the failure of the
father to cover her in proper authority and protection. We
thank You for a new day, a fresh start, and a new beginning
in Christ Jesus our Lord. Amen.

Let me assure you that if you received this spiritual transaction
and divine legal decree in your heart and life, then there's a
dynamic chain reaction of correction going up and down
throughout your bloodline in this moment. The Spirit of the living God is even pursuing things passed on to your children and
pulling them out in divine power.

I don't think you understand. There are curses that have been
destroyed, ways of life that have been shattered, and a spirit of
blessing replaces them.

Chapter 9

To Know

Every year, the makeup of America's church population seems to shift more and more toward single-parent, single-provider homes where children must make do with the best-effort parenting of half of God's best.

Many of us were raised in single-parent homes where *lack* was a constant companion and *plenty* our constant hope. More than any amount of money, clothing, or necessities, the millions of children in these homes wish they had a mommy *and* a daddy working and loving together.

Many times these situations were created by people who were in love enough to give their bodies to one another, but who weren't committed enough to take responsibility for a marriage. When God blessed them with a child (He will not rescind the ancient law of sowing and reaping for a couple in lust), the child was usually left uncovered by the bonds of a marriage and parental covenant.

To be candid, I've been working to remove the tentacles of

nearly forty-seven years' worth of pain and complication that came my way against my will during the first twelve years of my life—and I was the son of a preacher.

It is probably safe to say that many of the things you must work out of your life also came your way during childhood. I know a number of people far older than I am who are still trying to work out the painful issues inflicted on their spirits during the first few years of their lives.

We view sex so casually that the children born of our random liaisons become casualties of our own fractured lifestyles, and they enter life worse off than we were! Just think of the complex messes that they have to deal with in their lives, all because we were so irresponsible with the sex act (I can't say "lovemaking" because lust played a larger part than any form of love).

WE GRATIFY THE FLESH BY ANY MEANS, AT ANY COST

The bottom line is that it usually is nothing more or less than the gratification of the flesh by any means necessary and at any cost. The mantra of the moment always seems to be, "Give it to me now."

There is a more proper and much deeper biblical term for the act of sexual union. The King James Version and similar older versions translate the original Hebrew word *yada'* as "to know" or "knew."[1] "Now Adam *knew* Eve his wife, and she conceived and bore Cain, and said, 'I have acquired a man from the LORD'" (Gen. 4:1, emphasis mine).

As modern educated people, we like to write off this term as quaint and archaic. The truth is that to "know" is closer to the truth than any of us could possibly believe. One thing seems certain: You don't have to be a Bible scholar to know that God's term for married sexual union certainly means more than "indiscriminate copulation like a dog." (Apparently, this is the most accurate term for sex in the minds of modern educated people.)

We have already seen that some of the most serious problems in the body of Christ are rooted in erroneous thinking about the biblical roles of men and women in the context of marriage, home, the family, and God's order.

Human beings have a virtually inexhaustible ability to create and dwell upon vain and empty thoughts. Frankly, there seem to be more empty thoughts than pure thoughts in the body of Christ today.

TAUGHT TO THINK IN THE FLESH

In essence, we are taught to think in the flesh. We are taught to think worldly, but we are also supposed to act like Christians. No wonder it is so easy for us to slip back into the mainstream culture of the world the moment we leave the sheltered walls of our church buildings.

The only reason we are taught to think like pagans is that those doing the teaching don't read the Bible. God said in Romans 12:2, "Do not be conformed to this world, but be transformed by the *renewing of your mind*" (emphasis mine). The Word seems very specific about renewing the *mind,* not the liver or gall bladder.

God wasn't caught off guard by the media noise levels of modern culture. He knew we would be pressured by our culture to conform to ungodly standards. That is why He spoke so emphatically in His Word about renewing our minds.

We need to be renewed daily to combat the constant barrage of persuasive images, critical analyses, angry outbreaks, and seductive appeals that come our way via full-color billboards, endless cable and satellite-television channels, aggressive Internet-pornography pushers, popular gossip tabloids, and sexually explicit magazine covers and so-called soft pornography magazines cluttering the racks of nearly every convenience store and gas station in America.

STAND AGAINST THE TIDE IN THE PERFECT WILL OF GOD

The daily assault of ungodly images, sounds, and sensations can be overwhelming at times. More than at any other time in history, we must guard our minds, train them, transform them, and discipline them so we can stand against the tide and prove what is good and what is acceptable and what is the perfect will of God (Rom. 12:2). That is our whole mission.

The world is looking for someone to identify as a genuine son or daughter of God without relying on any outward markings, signs, uniforms, or odd behavior. I'm afraid the world is about to call off the search party in disappointment.

Here is the problem: We are doomed to walk in the flesh and not in the Spirit as long as we fail to understand who we are in

Christ. Even worse, we will walk in the flesh while actually believing we are in the Spirit. Doing this ruins our witness to the unsaved because they can easily tell the difference between a fake and the real thing.

We still suffer from an often fatal snake-borne virus carried over from Eve's first episode in the Garden of Eden. Our erroneous thinking (and adoption of the world's philosophies) has led to a deep-seated *selfishness* that permeates everything we say and do. Everything seems to revolve around "me" in our lives, and God wants nothing of it.

Satan's self-centered pride triggered the angelic rebellion in heaven, and it is having the same effect among men and women on earth. We have no choice. We must root out this selfishness in us and replace it with love.

Selfishness is rooted in our arrogance and determination to pursue fulfillment of our desires independent of God. That is the very reason we have so much pain today. In many cases, our selfishness has put us in the difficult places we are in right now. We have tried to satisfy something in our lives without God.

TROUBLE COMES WHEN WE DECIDE GOD IS LATE

Take a few moments to go back through the years of your life and the storerooms of your memory. Do you remember a time, a situation, or a circumstance in which you somehow moved ahead of God to pursue a strong need or desire? For most of us, trouble comes whenever we decide that God is late or just taking too long. You can count on this: Once you step in to "help" God, everything will begin to take a turn for the worst. This is especially true when the "help" involves marriage, romantic relationships, or sexual desires.

What does all of this have to do with the biblical term *to know?* Everything. Nothing is more complex or in need of God's direct intervention than our journeys from puberty to the altar to make a marriage covenant. After that, we need daily doses of divine grace to make the constant adjustments required in a successful marriage.

The Bible says that Adam *knew* Eve. Make no mistake: The act of sexual union as God intended it to be is the highest and deepest level of intimacy you will ever experience in your earthly experience, and it is exclusively reserved for the institution of marriage.

Marriage is God's idea, not the world's sometime on-again, off-again concept. Satan would never come up with anything involving such voluntary and exclusive commitment for the purpose of keeping a human marital relationship pure. It is the opposite of everything he stands for and works for. You can be sure that marriage did not come from the world or from the glittery casino district of Las Vegas.

The Effects of Sex Are Powerful and Far-Reaching

Sexual intercourse is so intimate and its effects on the human soul and spirit are so powerful and far-reaching that God declared it to be illegal in any context other than within the bonds of the marriage covenant!

A covenant is the earth's strongest and most binding legal agreement available between two parties. It takes nothing less than a *mutually binding covenant* to contain the tremendous power and potential risk of marital intimacy.

Good marriages thrive on intimacy, vulnerability, and implicit and unbroken trust between two life partners stretching over many decades. God's kingdom order demands that such intimacy—the closest earthly mirror of the divine intimacy enjoyed in the Godhead—be preserved under the strongest and most binding of earthly commitments.

Contrary to popular cultural trends, sexual intercourse is *not* okay just because you say, "But I love him," or "But we are going to get married someday." It is *not* okay just because you say, "He's handsome," or "She's fine."

(By the way, even "heathens" are learning to be careful about judging people based on outward appearance. In this age of cosmetic miracles and plastic wonders, half of that stuff ain't real anyway.)

Adam *knew* Eve. God has always intended that both the man and the woman should approach the marriage covenant as virgins. Most of the attention in previous generations was focused on the man but not the woman.

SOW YOUR "WILD OATS" (BUT NOT WITH MY DAUGHTER)

Now what really bothers me is the spiritually nearsighted father who tries to protect his daughter but encourages his son to go out and "sow his wild oats." If there are even two sons out there "sowing their oats," then someone's daughter is getting something.

The last time I checked, God's Word still said, "Do not be

deceived, God is not mocked; for *whatever a man sows,* that he will *also reap"* (Gal. 6:7, emphasis mine).

A wedding is a celebration of a holy covenant between a man and a woman under the covering of God, but we treat it like a trivial ring-exchange ceremony with a covered-dish meal afterward.

When the Jews held weddings in Jesus' day, those weddings were community celebrations. Weddings were big on the local social calendar, and everybody who was anybody showed up for the fun. All I can tell you is that the people sure seemed to be happy when Jesus showed up and saved the day when the wine ran out at the wedding in Cana of Galilee. Mary boldly told the servants at the wedding, "Whatever He says to you, do it."

I think Mary's one-line prescription is still our best opportunity to heal the sick marriages in the church and strengthen our strong marriages even more. (I'm not talking about the wine; I'm talking about being obedient to everything Jesus says we should do.)

DID YOU BRING YOUR EVIDENCE OF SEXUAL PURITY?

Sexual purity was an absolute must in the marriage covenant in ancient Jewish weddings. It was symbolized by the "token of virginity" required as evidence of a bride's purity on her wedding night.

Why was public proof of virginity so important under the old covenant? When a groom has sexual intercourse with his virgin bride, he will nearly always tear a delicate membrane that stretches across the opening of the vagina.

Normally, the hymen contains an opening just large enough to permit the proper flow of menses during menstruation, but not large enough for the passage of the penis. This is the membrane that is ruptured in the initial act of sexual intercourse, and a small amount of blood from the hymen comes into contact with the man's penis. This shedding of blood on the male genitalia and the bedding was considered a valid covenant token that a marriage had just been consummated.

In the eyes of God, you just got married even though there wasn't an altar and no one exchanged rings. Caterers aren't even necessary for the act to be sealed according to the heavenly hosts because of the *shedding of blood.*

Believe it or not, the parents of any Jewish woman consummating her marriage covenant on her wedding night supplied clean sheets or bedding material carefully prepared for the couple's first sexual union.

Although the people in biblical times held to far higher moral standards than we do today, they were also less prudish about such natural things as sexual relations on a wedding night. The entire wedding party would gather outside the couple's bedroom and wait until the newlyweds confirmed that they had physically consummated their union in marriage!

Just Smile and Hand Over Those Sheets— They're Holding the Elevator

Can you imagine what the folks at the local Holiday Inn, Best Western, or Sheraton Hotel would think if a wedding party of two hundred hung around outside the honeymoon suite until the newlywed couple stepped out into the hall with flushed faces and big smiles to hand over their bloodied bedsheets? I think you're getting the picture.

Those bloody sheets were a token or evidence of the bride's virginity and of the couple's successful consummation of their wedding vows. The consummation was important to the witnesses because it was understood that the wedding union was complete only when blood had been shed. Historically, no covenant could be "cut" without the shedding of blood.

It was so important that nobody went anywhere until consummation took place. The happy couple didn't get on a plane and fly to Hawaii, and they didn't leave and go off to some secluded love nest somewhere. First they had to take care of business right then and there—everybody was waiting for some good news. (Talk about pressure!)

Before the families of the bride and groom could go home, they had to know that this marriage was a legitimate and binding *blood* covenant that could not be lightly broken. Now you know why the "knowing" was (and is) so important.

A passage in Deuteronomy 22 describes the unlikely but potentially deadly consequences of failing to provide clear tokens of virginity, or of lying about a woman's virginity:

> If any man takes a wife, and goes in to her, and detests her, and charges her with shameful conduct, and brings a bad name on her, and says, "I took this woman, and when I came to her I found she was not a virgin," then the father and mother of the young woman shall take and bring out the evidence of the young woman's virginity to the elders of the city

at the gate. And the young woman's father shall say to the elders, "I gave my daughter to this man as wife, and he detests her. Now he has charged her with shameful conduct, saying, 'I found your daughter was not a virgin,' and yet these are the evidences of my daughter's virginity." And they shall spread the cloth before the elders of the city. Then the elders of that city shall take that man and punish him; and they shall fine him one hundred shekels of silver and give them to the father of the young woman, because he has brought a bad name on a virgin of Israel. And she shall be his wife; he cannot divorce her all his days. (Deut. 22:13–19)

So you see, before the bride and groom could start off on their honeymoon trip, the elders had to inspect the sheets. It was common in that day for parents to preselect a husband or wife for their child long before their child reached puberty.

This custom of parental matchmaking usually worked out, but evidently, there were young men who tried to beat the system and cry foul—*after* the wedding night experience, of course. Whenever a groom brought a false claim against his bride, he was putting her at great risk of death. Once the virgin's father produced proof of his daughter's virginity, the lying groom was penalized and ordered to pay up.

Cursed by Themselves, Judged by God

What about all of the "brothers" who take out fine young Christian ladies and then lie to their brothers back home who ask, "Did you do it?" If you say yes when you know the correct answer is no, then you have just cursed yourself. You brought shame to the name of that lady's family by claiming you did something that you didn't. Now you are carrying God's judgment on you. You need to know that.

> But if the thing is true, and evidences of virginity are not found for the young woman, *then they shall bring out the young woman to the door of her father's house, and the men of her city shall stone her to death with stones,* because she has done a disgraceful thing in Israel, to play the harlot in her father's house. So you shall put away the evil from among you. (Deut. 22:20–21, emphasis mine)

In those days, that meant your wedding day could be the happiest day of your life or the *last* day of your life! According to the Bible, the Virgin Mary was "espoused" or formally engaged to marry Joseph when she turned up pregnant by divine intervention. Mary literally faced a potential death sentence if Joseph chose not to go along with her divine pregnancy assignment from heaven. That puts the commitment and courage of Mary and Joseph in a totally different light.

While I have no intention of keeping a stoning pile out in the church parking lot, I do want you to see how far the modern church has wandered from God's kingdom standard of sexual and marital purity. We don't take commitment seriously.

DON'T PLAY HOUSE UNTIL
YOU'VE CUT A COVENANT

Maybe that is why Paul warned the men at Corinth, "When it looks like you're tempted to play house before you've cut the covenant and bloodied the sheets, then run!" That is not praying time, and it isn't the time to stand around and speak in tongues. It's time to run! If you don't and you mess up, then you might end up under a pile of stones or disgrace your entire family.

I know this isn't something that triggers hallelujahs, but it has to be said.

Why is God so hard on sexual impurity? Why does He create such fine-looking women and good-looking men and then say, "No, don't you touch that"?

It is simple. No one puts a plain rock or a brown paper sack in a safety-deposit box. Ordinary items are available everywhere, but valuables are hidden away and secured in safe surroundings.

The marriage bed is sacred and holy. For some reason, God chose the marriage relationship as His primary way of illustrating His relationship to the church. The marriage covenant is God's crown jewel on earth. He didn't leave it out in the open where just anyone could mess with it.

He set the marriage covenant apart and encircled with the fear of the Lord. No one can approach this treasure unless he or she pays the price for "the beginning of wisdom" (Prov. 9:10).

Our problem is that nobody has enough common sense to be afraid of God. That is about to change.

If we knew there were consequences, and if we actually

enforced the Old Testament penalties for infidelity under the new covenant, people wouldn't be fornicating as they do now.

The Dogs Are Loose in the Choir Loft Again!

Even churchgoing choir members think there are no consequences, so they act like dogs in heat and wave off every godly warning under the American banner of individual independence: "I'll do whatever I want. Stay out of my private business."

I'm sorry, but there is a Power who is higher than any earthly government, and there is a Throne set in the heavenlies that towers high above the highest ruling of the U.S. Supreme Court.

I've often wondered if the covenant breakers who sneak off to commit adultery in some cheap motel room ever notice that there's no "separation of church and state" when it comes to a hotel. Most rooms have a Bible.

Think about it: God pays no attention to walls, doors, curtains, or bedcovers. The God of the universe sees and remembers every deed we do and every idle word we speak—somehow I think He will remember every covenant-breaking sin committed at the Heartbreaker Hotel.

How many women are still recovering from unlawful uncovering by uncaring men who left them holding the bag of overwhelming circumstance and a responsibility they cannot handle?

I'm in sin if I do not require the church to rise up and enforce the spiritual and moral consequences of sexual promiscuity. We must make it clear that there are consequences to sin.

MEDIA ROLE MODELS HAWKING
LUST AND DESIRE

Our young people are being programmed by the entertainment media to gravitate toward role models hawking immorality, impurity, sexual perversion, violence, disrespect for women, the lust of the flesh, and the desires of the eye. Quick gratification is the order of the day.

The buck should stop at the immovable gates of God's kingdom. I called everyone together for a staff meeting recently and explained something the Lord had laid on my heart: "Our number one concern right now in this church is our youth and our children. Our generation has messed them up. Our divorces and hectic lifestyles have so uncovered them that there is nothing in them to help them stand."

We all need to *yada'* or to *know* the heart and will of God. We need to *know* one another well enough to cover one another in love and mutual care. We need to *know* the state of the flock God has given to each of us.

THIS FACTOR ALONE MAY CHANGE THE FUTURE

Finally, husbands and wives need to *know* each other in ways that foster mutual respect, love, honor, and joy in each other and in their homes. This single factor alone may well change the future of the next generation in the kingdom!

No matter what happened yesterday, there is only one way to move on from this point today. That is the way of repentance and forgiveness. Our hope and security are in the God we serve, the

God who is not like a man or woman. When He forgives our sins, He puts them under the blood of Jesus and throws them into the sea of forgetfulness.

That means He will forgive anything. Don't lose sleep at night and let the devil whisper in your ear, "God is not going to forgive you."

What you actually need is a dose of grace so you can forgive *yourself.* The Word of God declares:

> If we walk in the light as He is in the light, we have fellowship with one another, and *the blood of Jesus Christ His Son cleanses us from all sin.* If we say that we have no sin, we deceive ourselves, and the truth is not in us. If we confess our sins, *He is faithful and just to forgive us our sins and to cleanse us from all unrighteousness.* (1 John 1:7–9, emphasis mine)

Are you a man who longs to walk in sexual purity? Have you ever been disrespectful toward a woman? Are you tired of viewing women merely as sex objects? Do you have a son or daughter from a past liaison who doesn't live with you and for whom you have taken no responsibility?

This is your opportunity to get right with God and make things right with your own flesh and blood. Pray this prayer with me:

> *Father, in the name of Jesus, we lift up those sons and daughters wherever they are at this very moment. Step into*

their situations wherever they are and bring Your abundant
supply wherever they are lacking. As for me, Lord, I have come
to surrender my life and do what is right in Your sight.

Touch them, God. Give them the fullness of Your Spirit,
and touch them right now in the name of Jesus. Bring forth
every healing that they need in the name of Jesus. We thank
You for divine wholeness from the very crowns of their heads to
the soles of their feet. Heal their bodies, their souls, their
minds, and their spirits. Touch the loneliness they've felt since
they were little children. Touch the emptiness. Let them feel
their Father's love.

The Bible says that healing comes when we confess our sins one
to another. Find a brother whom you can trust to love you unconditionally, someone to whom you can confess your sin, knowing
he will pray with you and help you move on to new levels of maturity and joy. Healing comes in the midst of that process.

Now let me warn you: You can't tell *everybody* about your stuff.
Jesus saw something special in Peter, James, and John that the
rest of the disciples just didn't have. Even Jesus couldn't sit with
all twelve disciples and share everything on His heart. He chose
twelve for His daily ministry functions, but when He was ready
to talk about or reveal the more intimate personal things, He
seemed to trust only Peter, James, and John.

Brother, take your lead from Jesus. Find yourself a Peter, James,
and John. You don't have to gather together a big crowd of brothers—develop an intimate relationship with a Peter, James, or John.
They will help you walk in what God has ordained for you to do.

Do You Feel Uncomfortable
and Unclean in Some Way?

Sister, perhaps all of this talk about "proof of virginity" has made you feel very uncomfortable and unclean in some way. Perhaps you are feeling guilt from something that happened in the past. You serve the God of the Second Chance.

If Jesus can run off a crowd of angry men just so He can set free a woman caught in the act of adultery, if He can forgive the men who were crucifying Him, then I assure you, He is well able to remove that pain from your past.

Father, in Jesus' name I pray that You take my sister's guilt and shame from yesterday and remove it as far as the east is from the west. Restore to her everything that has been stolen from her—including her sense of purity. Give her a fresh start today, and plant a love in her heart that refuses to let her settle for less than Your very best for her life.

Chapter 10

PULLED ASIDE FOR A
DATE WITH DESTINY

M ost of us know the sinking feeling that hits the stomach. A mad rush of blood flows to your head and extremities as the thought flashes through your mind, *Pulled over again.*

The flashing blue lights and siren send an unmistakable signal to every cell in your body, and dread settles down over your mind and emotions. You have been arrested by the long arm of the law. Once again you've been pulled aside for a date with the ticket book and the uniformed man under the crisp hat brim.

I hope this doesn't happen very often in your life, but on the other hand, I hope it happens regularly in your journey through God's kingdom. Arrests are good things in the kingdom. God uses them to bring us Fatherly correction, instruction, and guidance. When the "flashing lights" of the Holy Spirit overtake your life and pull you over, you have proof that your heavenly Father favors you and loves you.[1]

The apostle Paul may be the best-known "arrestee" in the

Bible. He was Saul the high roller, the favored son among the religious elite of his day. He was the remarkable rookie, the MVP (Most Valuable Player) who launched a comeback of the "Sanhedrin Home Boys" against the upstart Christian farm team from the Galilee hood.

He was going for the all-time grand-slam mark for HBHs (heretics batted home) with the approving nod of the high priest commissioner when a flashing light from heaven temporarily blinded him. The Owner had pulled the wonder kid aside for a date with destiny.

When God's redirection program was complete, Saul had become Paul, and his years of study under the master rabbi Gamaliel had been replaced by three years of study under the Holy Spirit in the Arabian desert and in Damascus, Syria (Gal. 1:17–18).

From Saul the Super-Jew to Paul the Least of the Apostles

He was no longer Saul the Super-Jew, sent to lead the Jews in an anti-Christian campaign. He was Paul, the "least of the apostles," sent to preach Christ and the kingdom to lowly Gentiles or non-Jewish people throughout the known world.

As Saul, he had been trained by the hand of man to rule the religious halls of Jerusalem's temple of Herod. After his date with destiny, God sent Saul, known as Paul, into foreign nations to meet women washing their clothes. His assignment also included becoming a spiritual father to mixed-nationality orphan boys, jail keepers, and the house servants of Caesar himself.

At one time, Saul the Roman citizen and high-ranking rabbi could have ridden on the finest horses, ships, and conveyances money could buy. After his date with destiny, Paul experienced the less pleasant side of travel on kingdom business—he traveled in a basket to escape death, he was shipwrecked, and he traveled in cold weather and wet weather, and in Roman chains.

Before his encounter, Saul was probably destined to marry a well-placed Jewish woman of priestly blood and settle down for the good life in Jerusalem's highest circles of religious and social leadership. After he saw the light of divine arrest, Paul was destined to lay down his life for people he had been trained to despise in the name of a Master he had openly called a heretic.

What a man *really* wants is an encounter with the living God, an encounter that sets his life course to the "true north" of the kingdom and sets him on a journey into the Father's presence.

What a woman really needs isn't a date with a mere man; it is a date with destiny. She longs to meet the one Man who laid down His life for her, and will never leave or forsake her. Everything after that will look different in her eyes. Every man she meets after that must meet a much higher standard than he could ever reach on his own.

The three patriarchs of the Jewish people, Abraham, Isaac, and Jacob, had their own dates with destiny.

GOD SHOWED UP FOR A TALK ABOUT THE FUTURE

Abram the pagan was a moon worshiper, and the son of a moon worshiper from the land of Chaldee. He was happily married to a beautiful woman named Sarai, despite the obvious problem that his wife appeared to be infertile. Abram was set to take over his father's business until the day God showed up for a talk about his future and sent him to a place called Canaan.[2]

That little talk turned out to be Abram's first date with destiny—a date that directly affected *our* destiny as well. God promised Abram a son through Sarai, but that promise didn't even begin to come to pass for twenty-five years. Then his elderly wife suddenly came up pregnant as promised and gave birth to Isaac in Abram's one-hundredth year.

Their names were changed to Abraham and Sarah along the way, and the rest of the promise came to pass the day Jesus Christ was born in Bethlehem, when all nations were blessed through Abraham's seed.

Abraham and his son Isaac would face their most important date with destiny together on Mount Moriah, far from where Sarah waited for them. Some of our most difficult dates with destiny demand a supernatural trust in our fathers that may even defy logic.

> Now it came to pass after these things that God tested Abraham, and said to him, "Abraham!" And he said, "Here I am." Then He said, "Take now your son, *your only son* Isaac, *whom you love,* and go to the land of Moriah, and *offer him there as a burnt offering* on one of the mountains of which I shall tell you." (Gen. 22:1–2, emphasis mine)

As you and I read this, we enjoy the comfort of hindsight. We already know how everything turned out. Abraham knew only that the same God who promised him a son and worked a miracle to keep that promise was now commanding him to sacrifice Isaac.

HE HAD TO TRUST HIS FATHERLIKE
ONE AGAINST ALL LOGIC

Abraham also knew about the custom of human sacrifices among the followers of the bloodthirsty false gods of other nations, so he had to trust this heavenly Fatherlike One against all logic.

> Abraham took the wood of the burnt offering and laid it on Isaac his son; and he took the fire in his hand, and a knife, and the two of them went together. But Isaac spoke to Abraham his father and said, "My father!" And he said, "Here I am, my son." Then he said, "Look, the fire and the wood, but *where is the lamb* for a burnt offering?" And Abraham said, "My son, *God will provide for Himself the lamb* for a burnt offering." So *the two of them went together.* (Gen. 22:6–8, emphasis mine)

Isaac knew even less about what was going on, but we know from his life story that this young man wasn't stupid. He knew they were going to make a blood sacrifice somewhere, and the only thing missing was the sacrificial animal.

PURELY A MATTER OF TRUST

I'm sure Isaac also knew the custom of worshipers in the region to offer their firstborn children as blood sacrifices to appease

Molech. He knew his father's God only through his father at that point, so it was purely a matter of trust. That had to be the most difficult trip of his life, but the most difficult *moment*—the ultimate date with destiny—was still ahead of him.

> Then they came to the place of which God had told him. And Abraham built an altar there and placed the wood in order; and *he bound Isaac his son and laid him on the altar,* upon the wood. And Abraham stretched out his hand and *took the knife to slay his son.* (Gen. 22:9–10, emphasis mine)

That was the moment of truth, when the trust in their fathers was stretched to the breaking point (and the point of no return). Both the Father with the promise and the son of promise had arrived at the point where the death of their promise and their trust in fatherhood were about to die with the plunge of a knife. A date with destiny was in the making, and neither man flinched.

It appears that Isaac was a grown man at this time, while his father was well past the age of one hundred. The only way Abraham could have bound Isaac was for him to offer himself as a sacrifice willingly, just as another beloved Son would willingly sacrifice His life on that same mountain many generations later.

THE SACRIFICED LAMB FOR THE SON OF PROMISE

What went through their minds in that moment? No one but God really knows. We do know the rest of the story, however. Jesus appeared as "the Angel of the Lord" in that moment and spoke out on Isaac's behalf. The Sacrificed Lamb intervened for the first son of promise:

> "Do not lay your hand on the lad, or do anything to him; for now I know that you fear God, since *you have not withheld your son, your only son,* from Me." Then Abraham lifted his eyes and looked, and there behind him was a ram caught in a thicket by its horns. (Gen. 22:12–13, emphasis added)

Isaac's next date with destiny should give hope to every unmarried man or woman in the kingdom. Many years after the miracle on Mount Moriah and after Sarah had died, Abraham declared by faith that God would also provide a wife for his son of promise, who was then forty years old. (More parents in the kingdom should be taking this approach today.) He told the servant assigned to seek out a wife from Abraham's family living back in the land of Chaldee:

> The LORD God of heaven, who took me from my father's house and from the land of my family, and who spoke to me and swore to me, saying, "To your descendants I give this land," *He will send His angel before you,* and you shall take a wife for my son from there. (Gen. 24:7, emphasis mine)

ONE OF THE MOST DRAMATIC AND ROMANTIC SCENES

Evidently, even Abraham's servants had been infected by Abraham's faith in God. When the servant finally arrived at the city of Nahor in Mesopotamia, he prayed and asked for God's help in choosing the woman preordained by God to be Isaac's wife. Just as he completed the prayer, he saw Rebekah walk to the well for water. After a series of events, we see one of the most dramatic and romantic scenes in the Scriptures: "Isaac went out to meditate in the field in the evening; and he lifted his eyes and looked, and there, the camels were coming. Then Rebekah lifted her eyes, and when she saw Isaac she dismounted from her camel" (Gen. 24:63–64).

What does every man want? The woman God intends for him and a meaningful relationship with God. What does every woman need? A godly man who seeks the face of God in the evening and trusts Him for every good thing, and her own personal relationship with the heavenly Father.

When it became apparent that Rebekah was barren, Isaac asked God for the same medical miracle received by Abraham and Sarah. The Lord answered his prayer, and Rebekah gave birth to twins, Esau and Jacob.

Jacob the trickster seems to be a perfect match with many of the young men who play the singles game in America today. His life was filled with misadventures and errors of the flesh and human nature, but our interest for this book focuses on two events in his life.

Seven Years Were As a Few Days Because of Love

The first event began when Jacob fell in love with a woman named Rachel. Her father, Laban, promised Jacob her hand in marriage if he would work for him over a period of years. The

Bible tells us, "So Jacob served seven years for Rachel, and *they seemed only a few days to him* because of the love he had for her" (Gen. 29:20, emphasis mine). This is the kind of love every kingdom woman wants and needs.

Rachel's father fooled Jacob on his wedding night and actually substituted Rachel's older sister, Leah, instead. Then he bargained with Jacob to work *another period of seven years* for Rachel, and Jacob accepted.

There is something holy and right about a man paying a dear price and making a costly sacrifice to win the woman of his dreams. It should *still* be that way.

A kingdom man must be willing to commit his life to a woman in marriage *before* he ever entertains the idea of becoming intimate with her. This is true kingdom covenant in action. We don't date to marry; we marry to date our spouses.

A Permanent Limp and a New Identity

Jacob's greatest date with destiny began later during a celestial wrestling match, and he ended with a permanent limp and a new identity.

> Then Jacob was left alone; and a Man wrestled with him until the breaking of day. Now when He saw that He did not prevail against him, He touched the socket of his hip; and the socket of Jacob's hip was out of joint as He wrestled with him. And He said, "Let Me go, for the day breaks." But he said, "I will not let You go unless You bless

me!" So He said to him, "What is your name?" He said, "Jacob." And He said, *"Your name shall no longer be called Jacob, but Israel; for you have struggled with God and with men, and have prevailed."* Then Jacob asked Him, saying, "Tell me Your name, I pray." And He said, "Why is it that you ask about My name?" And He blessed him there. And Jacob called the name of the place Peniel: "For *I have seen God face to face*, and my life is preserved." Just as he crossed over Penuel *the sun rose on him, and he limped on his hip.* (Gen. 32:24–31, emphasis mine)

Jacob's encounter with divine destiny transformed him from Jacob the heel catcher and trickster into Israel, a prince of God. His limp became a permanent reminder of the day he came face-to-face with the Lord and was changed. The same One who transformed Jacob is waiting for His appointment with *you.*

Does Spelling Your Name Correctly Count for Anything?

I took a basic aptitude test in the seventh grade, and during a review of the results, my guidance counselor (I remember his full name to this day) asked me what I wanted to be. When I told him I had always dreamed of becoming a lawyer, he said, "According to your test results, you can't be a lawyer." Then he asked me what my father did, and I said he was a preacher and a mechanic. He said, "Well, you can probably be one of those."

After that uplifting experience, all interest in school died. I remained in school only because of my interest in sports. Another guidance counselor grabbed and "arrested" me in the twelfth grade, and she basically made me take the SAT. Since I'd had no academic interest since the seventh grade, my SAT scores weren't impressive. I think I received the top score earned for those able to correctly spell their names at the top of the test sheet. It didn't matter to this counselor—she looked beyond where I was to what I could become.

It was a miracle for me even to be accepted in a college program. I know God was at work behind the scenes, arranging my date with destiny through miraculous intervention. The miracle continued to expand as I majored in business and marketing and ultimately graduated with a B average. Yet through it all, I still had this longing to be a lawyer. I finally took the graduate school entrance exam for law school, and I can still remember the day I was told I had missed the requirement by a fraction of a point. I literally wept on the steps of the law school all day long.

My grief was so intense that day that I didn't care who saw me crying. It was my senior year of college. Although I'd taken a lot of trips to interview with prospective employers, no one had offered me a job. I was delivering newspapers every day from twelve midnight to six o'clock in the morning. All of my dreams and hopes had been destroyed.

Arrested and Catapulted into God's Perfect Will

I eventually landed a job with Ford Motor Company and then went through an unwanted and heartbreaking divorce. God was faithful through it all, and somehow He used my impossible circumstances to rearrange my destiny that catapulted me into His perfect will in the ministry. He arrested me and put me in college when I shouldn't have been there. When I tried to apply for additional college education to become a lawyer, He stopped me. Why?

He wanted me to become a *greater* lawyer for the law firm of Father, Son, and Holy Spirit. I argue cases every day for the souls of men, women, and children. In a sense, I'm better than Perry Mason, and I'm better than Johnny Cochran (although he is a friend who said one day he would allow me to close a case for him). I'm better because I don't argue just one case at a time. When I preach to my congregation and reach out through the electronic media to people around the world, I'm seeking to influence multiple souls and getting them started on the right course. There is no better joy than to actually fulfill my destiny as an advocate of the kingdom, saving the lost of the world.

It was God who arrested me and led me down a path, even though I was totally lost. Now I'm walking into the future with no regrets.

Whether you are married or single, you will never be "all you can be" until you have a date with destiny and allow God to transform and reform you according to His kingdom purposes. Seek Him, obey Him, yield to the Holy Spirit, and allow Him to mold you into the man or woman He has called you to be.

Moses entered life under dramatic circumstances, and his life was spared under even more miraculous conditions. Yet he was destined to experience countless dates with destiny in the process of becoming the man God intended for him to be.

If you were born anytime after the wholesale practice of abortion on demand came under the protection of the U.S. Supreme Court, you are a miracle child. By God's grace, you escaped our nation's federally endorsed infanticide campaign and lived to tell about it.

TOTAL FAILURE CATAPULTED HIM OUT FROM UNDER THE INFLUENCE

Adopted by Pharaoh's daughter, Moses was trained in Pharaoh's household as a prince of Egypt, but even that highly advanced education for leadership fell short of his destiny in God. It took total failure to catapult him out from under forty years of Pharaoh's influence and into the wilderness for another forty years of training for his date with destiny.[3]

It was during this wilderness period that Moses met and married Zipporah, the dark-skinned daughter of the priest of Midian.[4] Moses' training in the wilderness didn't take place in a school for princes or a seminary for preachers.

HE STUMBLED UPON HIS DESTINY WHILE TENDING ANOTHER MAN'S SHEEP

Moses stumbled into his date with destiny while tending his father-in-law's sheep—something any respectable Egyptian despised as the lowest of all vocations:

Now Moses was tending the flock of Jethro his father-in-law, the priest of Midian. And he led the flock to the back of the desert, and came to Horeb, the mountain of God. And *the Angel of the LORD* [commonly understood to be the preincarnate Christ] *appeared to him in a flame of fire from the midst of a bush.* So he looked, and behold, the bush was burning with fire, but the bush was not consumed. Then Moses said, "I will now turn aside and see this great sight, why the bush does not burn." So when the LORD saw that he turned aside to look, God called to him from the midst of the bush and said, "Moses, Moses!" And he said, "Here I am." Then He said, "Do not draw near this place. Take your sandals off your feet, for the place where you stand is holy ground." (Ex. 3:1–5, emphasis mine)

Moses stumbled into his date with destiny while doing what most of us do most of the time—he was faithfully tending to another man's business and goods. Jesus said, "If you have not been faithful in what is another man's, who will give you what is your own?" (Luke 16:12).

Moses had been faithful to tend Jethro's sheep and be a husband to Jethro's daughter for forty years. It was at the burning bush of destiny that God entrusted *His* sheep and *His spiritual* daughter to Moses for the next forty years. He went on to confront Pharaoh, witness the destruction of Egypt's army, lead the children of Israel out of Egypt, and guide them in a forty-year trek through the wilderness. Are you being faithful with everything that has been placed in your hand?

RUTH HAD THREE STRIKES AGAINST HER, BUT DESTINY WAS WAITING

God establishes His kingdom and accomplishes His purposes using both men and women in partnership. Ruth was a woman, a widow, and a Moabite, so according to ancient cultural customs, she had three big strikes against her when she left her homeland to follow her mother-in-law, Naomi, back to Bethlehem.

All Ruth knew was that her mother-in-law and mentor served a God who made her different somehow. She sensed destiny in her relationship with Naomi, and it led her to defy logic and follow her mentor wherever she went. Her kingdom declaration is considered one of the supreme models of kingdom-covenant relationship in the Bible:

> [Naomi] said, "Look, your sister-in-law has gone back to her people and to her gods; return after your sister-in-law."
> But Ruth said:
> "Entreat me not to leave you,
> Or to turn back from following after you;
> For *wherever you go, I will go;*
> *And wherever you lodge, I will lodge;*
> *Your people shall be my people,*
> *And your God, my God.*
> Where you die, I will die,
> And there will I be buried.
> The LORD do so to me, and more also,
> *If anything but death parts you and me."* (Ruth 1:15–17, emphasis mine)

Ruth's covenant speaks of a marriage of spirit between a daughter and her motherlike one. It is so powerful and anointed that elements of her faith declaration have found their way into countless wedding vows over the ages and for good reason. Just as spiritual sons must trust their fathers in times of crisis, so must spiritual daughters trust their mothers in crucial encounters with destiny.

How Do You Launch the Dreams of God?

Ruth carefully followed the counsel of her mother-in-law after they arrived in Bethlehem. That released God to carefully engineer a marriage made in heaven as He delivered to Boaz the wife he wanted and gave Ruth the godly husband she desperately needed. It is this kind of submission in kingdom-covenant relationship that launches the dreams of God and overcomes every obstacle thrown in the way.

Although Naomi and Ruth arrived in Bethlehem destitute and virtually without hope in the natural, God was leading them to a date with destiny that would transform their future and prepare the way for the coming of the Messiah. Ruth's union in marriage to Boaz produced a son named Obed. Later on, Obed had a son named Jesse, and Jesse in turn had a son named David, who became the king of Israel.

David didn't start out in the palace of a king; he was another one that God sent to the "school of the lambs" to prepare for his date with destiny. God prepared David's heart for leadership under the gentle influence of His presence through intimate worship. That personal relationship with God let David understand who he really was, despite the fact that he was the youngest child in a large family on the back side of nowhere.

This young boy's intimacy with God translated into the kind of supernatural power and courage that empowered him to kill a marauding bear and a lion barehanded when they attacked his father's sheep.

His True Baptism in Obedience Took Place in a Cave

David's early preparation helped him defeat Goliath in open combat armed only with the declaration of faith and the tools of a shepherd (1 Sam. 17:39–40). David experienced an early encounter with destiny when Samuel the prophet anointed him as King Saul's replacement, but it seems his true baptism in obedience took place in a cave.

David had a great promise and prophecy to hold on to, but he had to run for his life for many years before he saw that promise come to pass. During those years, many of them spent in "the cave Adullam," he perfected the art of praise and worship. It appears that many of the psalms were written in the darkness of that cave, and it was there that David learned how to transform fractured and disheartened men into skilled warriors and faithful kingdom men.

Some dates with destiny occur in the twinkling of an eye (it happened that way in Paul's life). Others, as in David's case, may last for many years. Either way, the goal is still the same: to enter into God's kingdom purposes and fulfill your destiny in Him.

Be careful about looking for shortcuts if you find yourself in a long-term date with destiny. I wrote in my book *Taking Over:*

> While God is working to mature the people in His church by allowing them to walk through various trials, His less-discerning ministers and pastors try to preach the people out of those trials! The problem is that when people listen to that kind of preaching and start begging God for a quick fix to their long-term problem, they just might get what they are asking for.[5]

I'M SURE GLAD JESUS DIDN'T TAKE A SHORTCUT

I know of one person who endured more pain and suffering than anyone else I can think of. I'm sure glad He didn't take a shortcut or ask God for the easy way out. Jesus experienced the greatest and most painful of all dates with destiny.

His success made us all successful, and His pain made it possible for us to endure every pain life brings us. Above all, His death freed us from the grip of death, and His resurrection brought new life to everyone who receives Him as King and Savior.

Consider these two Scripture passages. The first encourages us to follow the King's example and be encouraged. In the second, the apostle Paul described the certainty of God's faithfulness and the certainty of persecution if you choose to live as a kingdom person in a world that does not recognize God's kingdom.

> We also, since we are surrounded by so great a cloud of witnesses, let us lay aside every weight, and the sin which

so easily ensnares us, and let us run with endurance the race that is set before us, looking unto Jesus, the author and finisher of our faith, *who for the joy that was set before Him endured the cross, despising the shame,* and has sat down at the right hand of the throne of God. For consider Him who endured such hostility from sinners against Himself, *lest you become weary and discouraged* in your souls. (Heb. 12:1–3, emphasis mine)

You have carefully followed my doctrine, manner of life, purpose, faith, longsuffering, love, perseverance, persecutions, afflictions, which happened to me at Antioch, at Iconium, at Lystra—what persecutions I endured. And *out of them all the Lord delivered me.* Yes, and all who desire to live godly in Christ Jesus *will suffer persecution.* (2 Tim. 3:10–12, emphasis mine)

Whether you are married or single, a man or a woman, today marks another date with destiny in your life. This is your opportunity to make a kingdom choice. If you dare to follow the King wherever He leads you, I assure you the cost will be well worth the benefit of His perfect love.

· *Chapter 11* ·

PASSION FOR LIFE

The saddest thing you could ever do is to die having never truly lived. On a typical Sunday, the odds are very high that you are sitting next to somebody who has *never* truly lived. Do you understand what I'm talking about?

SURROUNDED BY FIRE KILLERS

There is a fire that burns in me. The best way to describe it to you is to say that I want to meet God and hear Him tell me, "Eddie, you did it *all.* Everything I spoke to you, you did! You left *nothing* undone. Well done, My good and faithful servant."

I don't want to leave this life and hear Him say, "Eddie, now look at all of this that I had for you. Son, *you didn't even live.*" Do you think this sounds overly spiritual? Think of the time Jesus described Himself with these words: "The thief does not come except to steal, and to kill, and to destroy. I have come that they may have life, and that they may have it more abundantly" (John 10:10).

Every day you awaken with the gift of breath, life presents you with an important choice: *Will you live for Him, or will you live for yourself this day?* Too many men and women waste their days in mindless pursuit of what they *think* they want or need. And even more married and single Christians have quit and disqualified themselves because of their *sins*.

I will never forget the time a young unwed mother stood up before thousands of people during a Father's Day church service to say something we rarely hear in church these days:

"Even though I have sinned, I am not disqualified. Even though things have gone on in my life that should never have happened, God is still using me. And I'm going to be a good mama, and he's going to be a good daddy. And this child shall be all that God ordained!"

Some of us have allowed failure to effectively end our lives! The truth is that everybody has challenges, failures, temptations, and difficulties to endure in life. It seems that we are always staging impromptu "pain fests" when we get together.

MY PAIN IS WORSE THAN YOUR PAIN!

Everybody digs for the worst story and the sorriest sorrow in life in a contest to see who has gone through the most sorrow. Really, it just doesn't matter if we can't testify about what God did in those situations. The only thing the King is interested in is how many of *His* things we picked up and ran with in spite of our weaknesses and failures.

No matter who you are, what title you carry, or how much

money you have in your pocket and bank account, you will always face some sin-and-failure stuff to jump over, move aside, or press through.

Don't take my word for it. Jesus is the One who said, "These things I have spoken to you, that in Me you may have peace. *In the world you will have tribulation;* but be of good cheer, *I have overcome the world*" (John 16:33, emphasis mine).

Now I want you to examine three brief Scripture passages before we go on:

> We also, since *we are surrounded by so great a cloud of witnesses,* let us lay aside every weight, and the sin which so easily ensnares us, and let us run with endurance the race that is *set* before us. (Heb. 12:1, emphasis mine)

> Behold, *I have refined* [or *chosen*] *you,* but not as silver; I have *tested you in the furnace* of affliction. (Isa. 48:10, emphasis mine)

> Then I arose in the night, I and a few men with me; I told no one *what my God had* put *in my heart* to do at Jerusalem; nor was there any animal with me, except the one on which I rode. (Neh. 2:12, emphasis mine)

DISCOVER THE POWER OF PASSION

If you catch this truth, your life will be changed. You need to discover the power of passion and how it relates to the destiny that God *put* in you. Destiny isn't an accident; it is a divine decree waiting for you to arrive.

Bill Russell was probably one of the greatest basketball players who ever lived. He played for the NBA's Boston Celtics during their heyday, and one of his chief rivals was Wilt Chamberlain.

When commentators talk about Bill Russell, certain characteristics consistently surface in their comments: He always gave 110 percent effort in a game, and his passion was evident in everything he did. I discovered an expression Bill Russell used throughout his career, and he even posted it over his locker area where he read it before every game: "The game is scheduled. I must play it, so I might as well win."

I adapted that saying for my own use, and I think of it every morning to ignite my passion and get my blood moving: "Life is scheduled. I have to live it; therefore, I might as well win."

Many of us do not truly live because we do not operate with *passion.*

"What do you mean, Bishop?"

We do not operate with passion because most of us feel like complete failures.

Let me put something in perspective: If the truth be told, your neighbor has failed in a whole lot of stuff too. Just look at the people around you. Look at your boss. Look at your preacher. Look at your most trusted friends. No matter how hard they try, they are still terminally human. Everywhere you look—you are looking at a failure.

The same would be true if you could look at me right now. I assure you that before this day is out, before I lay my head down to sleep, I will fail.

I might as well just say it: Just as sure as you breathe and exhale, you are destined to fail. Yet there is something divine that God put inside you that transcends and overcomes every kind of failure you will ever experience in this life . . . *if* you don't concede to the mess!

I praise God for that young unwed mother who openly admitted to my congregation:

"Well, we had this baby and we weren't married. But I thank God that failure isn't final! I thank God that He is faithful and just.

"Because He got me up this morning, something inside me says, 'It ain't over.' And I'm determined not to allow my child to suffer because I made a mistake.

"I'm going to stand and tell the world, because if God still be for me (and last time I checked He is), then who in the world can stand against me?"

Pardon my English, but I have to say it the way I have to say it:

It ain't over until it's over—and it still ain't over
because God *put* something in me!

The problem with most of us is, we don't know what He *put* in us. When God puts a thing in someone, there isn't any accident, coincidence, or happenstance involved.

Our ignorance of what God *put* in us has a serious consequence. It means there is nothing in us that motivates us to succeed. We resemble a race car with incredible potential—without any fuel we are reduced to a useless pile of metal and plastic. We are all dressed up on the outside with no gas for the pass to the fast lane.

That *put* from God causes us to have passion. I read somewhere that 50 percent of the CEOs running the Fortune 500 companies had a C or a C-minus average in school. Seventy-five percent of the men who have served as president of the United States were ranked in the *lower half* of their school percentile! Fifty percent of all millionaires never went to college, or if they did, they just dropped out early without earning a college degree.

THE FIRE IN THEM DEFIED THE STATISTICS

Why did I bring up those statistics? You and I need to understand that your success or failure usually has nothing to do with your job or your education! However, it has *everything* to do with what God *put* in you. I guarantee you that all of the individuals who defied the statistics and excelled in business, politics, and world leadership had a *fire* in them!

Let me give you one more name: Jeremiah. This Old Testament prophet was able to put words to his situation:

> I said, "I will not make mention of Him,
> Nor speak anymore in His name."
> But His word was in my heart *like a burning fire*
> *Shut up in my bones;*
> *I was weary of holding it back,*
> *And I could not.*
> For I heard many mocking:

"Fear on every side!"

"Report," they say, "and we will report it!"

All my acquaintances watched for my stumbling, saying,

"Perhaps he can be induced;

Then we will prevail against him,

And we will take our revenge on him."

But the LORD is with me as a mighty, awesome One.

Therefore my persecutors will stumble, and will

    not prevail.

They will be greatly ashamed, for they will not prosper.

Their everlasting confusion will never be forgotten.

    (Jer. 20:9–11, emphasis mine)

Jeremiah said God's Word, that holy *put* of passion from heaven, was like a "burning fire" in his bones. What about you? Is anything burning inside your heart?

You should know that there are two things that dictate your success:

1. Your attitude (or how you think)
2. Your emotions (or how you feel)

If you can get your thinking right and your feelings right at the same time, nothing can stop you. If hell can't hold you down, then you will be a success in everything. Now do you understand why God tells you in His Word how to think and control your emotions? "If I can just *think* about His goodness . . . even if I fall, if I can just think about how good God is . . ."

Everybody seems to be busy thinking low. I'm sick of low-thinking people. God hasn't lost His power. He hasn't turned into the wimp of heaven, so we must look closer to home for the real problem. It is obvious that low-thinking people haven't spent enough time with God to know who they are or for what cause God brought them to this place.

God wants us to take our cue from our King. When Pilate asked Him if He was really a king, Jesus didn't hesitate because He had settled the issue in consultation with His Father:

> Pilate therefore said to Him, "Are You a king then?" Jesus answered, "You say rightly that I am a king. *For this cause I was born, and for this cause I have come into the world, that I should bear witness to the truth.* Everyone who is of the truth hears My voice." (John 18:37, emphasis mine)

FOR THIS CAUSE I HAVE COME

Are you one of those people who don't even know why they are here? You should be able to wake up every morning and say, "For *this cause* I was born." You should boldly answer every challenge from man or devil, "For *this cause* I have come into the world, that I should bear witness to the truth."

When you have a passion for the kingdom, people around you just don't have the option to be lukewarm with you. When you are passionate, they will love you, or they will hate you. Why? They will love you because you get them fired up, or they will hate you because they know you are going somewhere and they aren't.

The "haters" have a problem with you because they are too lazy to get up and go with you. Now they will talk about you endlessly, but no matter how long they talk or how much they wish you would shut up, they will hear the same thing every morning when you wake up: "For *this cause* God brought me here! I am here to bring life!"

One of the biggest problems we face in our churches is that we have surrounded ourselves with "fire killers" and self-appointed "wet blankets." All these people want to talk about is *their pain.* We might as well put them all together in one Sunday school class and call them "Major Pain."

I'm sorry, but I don't want to hear about what you've been through. I want to talk about what you've *produced!*

Every woman who has ever given birth to a child knows exactly what I'm talking about. Your body went through all kinds of physical changes for nine months. You endured the excruciating pain of labor—*and it wasn't for you.*

WHERE IS THE PRODUCT OF YOUR PASSIONATE LABOR?

Mama, all of the pain and discomfort you went through was for *one cause*: You were determined to deliver that child of God from your womb. The moment that baby entered the world, all of the pain lost its power to hold your attention. All you were interested in was the *product* of your passionate labor.

Do you realize why God brought you here? He brought you here to give birth to His kingdom on earth as it is in heaven. He is stretching you, planting destiny, passion, and vision in your spiritual womb so you can press through the labor pains of life and bring something holy into this dark world. We were brought here for one holy cause: to birth something on earth that blesses others!

Your life isn't about you! Your life is about being a success so others can live. You are alive so you can tell others about how God *put* something in you and used you in spite of your failure. Tell the world there is life after divorce. There is life after sin. There is life after jail. But make sure you tell them that God gives the life!

Tell them, "I feel like I've been to hell and back again, but man didn't bring me back. It was God who brought me back and set me up on my feet. It was God who put this fire in me!"

"Behold, *I have refined* [or *chosen*] *you*, but not as silver; I have *tested you in the furnace* of affliction" (Isa. 48:10, emphasis mine). God is saying, "I have chosen you. I am testing you in the furnace of failure. Don't worry. I was *putting* something in you while I was *burning* something out of you."

God's Kids Were Making Him Look Bad

If you read the forty-eighth chapter of Isaiah, you will discover that God was angry with Israel because the entire nation had become a rebellious embarrassment to Him. They were such a sorry witness for God that He had to keep showing up just to set the record straight about Himself. His kids were making Him look so bad that He had to show up "for His name's sake."

Finally, God got tired of the merry-go-round. He was saying, "I'm sick of showing up when you should be showing out for Me. So what I'm going to do is *choose* you. I'll fix your problem in the furnace of affliction."

That was the ultimate woodshed, and the people of Israel were about to get a spanking from the Father of Lights that they would never forget. He was saying, "I'm going to put the pressure on you because I want you to show the world an accurate picture of what I really look like."

"It Ain't the Devil—It's God"

Listen, my friend—you've been chosen in the fire of God. That is why your life has been so hot. That is why things seem so confusing at times—He just lifted His hand and let you stumble in the dark for a while. That is why you have been falling down and tripping and going through this one blunder after another. At least you can take comfort from one fact: "It ain't the devil—it's God." He is saying:

"I chose you. I had to burn off some friends who were jealous of Me. I had to burn off some of those cars that were driving you away from Me.

"I had to burn away some of the flesh and barbecue some of those worldly mind-sets that made you think you know more than I do. I had to turn up the heat to burn away some tradition.

"Don't be dismayed because the fires are still burning. I won't stop until the process is complete and you are whole. It's okay because I have chosen you—whether you like it or not.

"I chose you, I snatched you from the flames of hell, and I put you into the purifying furnace of heaven. I had to remove your job; it was a distraction from the evil one.

"For that matter, I had to move aside or remove whatever you put before Me—including that ungodly man you loved more than Me. I knew you loved and trusted in the money more than you trusted in Me, so now you are bankrupt for a season. Fear not. For I have *chosen* you."

God says to each one of us: "I have sent you to accomplish something on this earth that *is bigger than you are.*"

Don't bother to offer Him some weak excuse about how it is too much for you. He chose Nehemiah to rebuild the walls that once encircled and protected the city of Jerusalem. There was at least one very big problem with the plan in the eyes of man: Nehemiah wasn't a contractor. He was a "food taster" by trade and training.

THE FOOD-TASTING PROPHET HAD A PASSION

Nehemiah's daily duty was to taste the king's food and taste the king's wine to make sure he wasn't secretly poisoned by his enemies. Yet when God *put* in him what He wanted done, nothing could stop Nehemiah from doing what God ordained. He had a passion, and that passion bled to the people, and the people rose up and built the walls!

Most of us never get anything done in the kingdom because we just sit there and try to figure out whether we can do it. Imagine that: The moment God drops something into our hearts, we try to tell God we can't do it!

I want you to know that even if you aren't trained in a thing, if God says that is what He wants you to do, then all you need to do is just show up. God puts you in a position, and then He trains you. Just show up with a burning heart. Just show up, and let the fire of God flame up with passion. That is what He needs from you. God will provide everything you need from that point on.

Remember, it isn't about you. There are lives weighing in the balance, and they are waiting for you to become the man or woman God ordained you to be. Don't worry if the fire in your life seems really hot at the moment—God is working in you to get you straight.

When God chooses you and tells you to do something, don't expect Him to change His mind. He isn't like us. If He says you are going to do it and go through it, then that is exactly what is going to happen. He won't take your no as an acceptable answer, and He won't pass over you. He refuses to get somebody else. Just ask Jonah. He'll tell you, "You can try to run; you can catch the first freighter to Joppa, but He will catch up with you."

WHAT IS YOUR TOP PRIORITY?

You have no choice once you've heard the call of God to a kingdom assignment. Once He *puts* a passion in you, then the pursuit of His purpose becomes your top priority. The call and passion of God have nothing to do with how much you get paid. They have nothing to do with the "career path" somebody prepared for you. (And this call is *not* limited to the people who feel they are called to pastor a church or proclaim the gospel full-time as evangelists.)

If you are really saved, then there is something inside you that gets you excited when you hear God's call. The big problem comes around seven o'clock on Sunday night when you start getting depressed because Monday is coming.

Why don't you like Mondays? Because you don't like the job you are committed to for five days out of every week. Again, you ask *why.* Because your weekly job doesn't have anything to do with what *God called you to do.* Five days a week you are doing something other than what you were born to do, and you hate it. It is no wonder you are usually late for work.

Listen, I don't have a *job*—I have a *life.* I love doing what God called me to do. It doesn't have anything to do with "the ministry." My joy comes from my obedience to God's will for my life.

You only have one life to live, so why don't you do something that you enjoy Monday through Sunday? Do something that brings glory to the kingdom, something that you do successfully. Once you find your place in the kingdom, people will have to *make* you stop pursuing your calling long enough to rest and eat!

Are there things God has *told* you to do that you won't move into? What are you doing now? Does it bring you joy and fulfillment? If not, then I suspect you are "hanging out for the money."

WHAT ARE YOU FOLLOWING?

It is time to take an inventory of your life. Our faith is out of joint if you and most of the other people in your church hate what they do most of the week! Why would we want to live longer when we don't even live the life we have? When you put this book down, subtract five days from every week that you have lived and find out how many days you actually have enjoyed.

I used to have a problem preaching to my congregation because I could see how substandard my life, my example, and my preaching were from the standards I'd set for myself (and those my congregation had set for me). Finally, I understood.

Don't Talk Your Way Out of God's Greatness

Most of us will talk our way right out of the greatness He has deposited in us because of the lives we live. I just want to encourage you to get into passion and don't talk yourself out of God's divine purpose for your life. It is a process, not instant perfection.

When my son graduated from high school, we celebrated his graduation together because that was the *purpose* for which I had sent him to school. Now my son wasn't perfect, but he still graduated. We were more interested in the fulfillment of the *purpose* for attending school than in any false measure of perfection.

If we had waited for my son to be perfect before he could advance from one grade to another, then he would have never finished school! If you are trying to be perfect before you move in your destiny, you will never accomplish what God ordained for you to do. There is something bigger going on here than your psychological need to get everything done.

God is saying to all of us, "Let Me in. I stand at the door and knock. Let Me in. If you get filled with Me, then you won't have to worry. I'm in charge now" (my free paraphrase of Luke 13:25).

The writer of the book of Hebrews said, "We also, since *we are surrounded by so great a cloud of witnesses,* let us lay aside every weight, and the sin which so easily ensnares us, and let us run with endurance the race that is *set* before us" (Heb. 12:1, emphasis mine).

THE HEROES OF FAITH ARE REALLY THE "CHARACTERS" OF FAITH

The twelfth chapter of Hebrews is actually a natural extension of the previous chapter that features a list of "witnesses" or heroes of faith. When I looked closely at the "heroes of faith" listed there, I felt inspired! I discovered whom God really uses! Consider some of the characters in God's roll call of faith and a good report:

- Noah was a drunk, an alcoholic who had to have folks "drive him home." He earned a good report *even though* . . .
- Abraham was a big-time liar who told a foreign king looking for a wife that Sarah was his sister! Yet he became known as the father of faith and earned a good report.
- Sarah literally sought out and hooked up another woman with her husband, Abraham, in a faithless effort to "help God" keep His promise of producing a male heir. The entire world, and the Middle East in particular, is still reeling from Sarah's fumbling efforts to help God. The descendants of Isaac (the Jewish people) are constantly battling the descendants of Ishmael (the Arab nations).
- Isaac, for his part, was a liar in the tradition of his father, Abraham. He also told men of whom he was afraid that Rebekah was his sister, with embarrassing results.
- Jacob was a born deceiver, a trickster, and a "shucker and a jiver." Nobody trusted him until *God* . . .
- Joseph, one of Jacob's sons, was a big-time bragger who told his brothers they would bow down to him. (If my brother

told me that, I'd throw him in a pit too.) Yet his life provides vivid proof that God can still use a bragger like you!

- Moses was a murderer who was never brought to trial or convicted. He was also disobedient to God (when he struck the rock with his staff instead of speaking to it as God commanded). Yet God still used him!
- Rahab was a harlot, or a whore, from the pagan city of old Jericho. Yet God still used her, and He even included her by name in the Messiah's family tree.

God takes special pains to find scarred people who have been in the fire and flame of human failure. They know the smell of the gutter and the glory of God's grace.

God isn't looking for perfect people because they don't exist (the only One left the "building" about two thousand years ago). He's looking for people who have learned to repent of their sins and walk through the process of restoration to kingdom success.

Great ministry is birthed out of the womb of pain and shame! If you're able to rise up from your shame when you hear God calling you, then He will use you! Just make sure you don't disqualify yourself by listening to what other people are saying. (Stick with the Word of God and you will be fine.)

DON'T LET PAST FAILURES KILL YOUR PASSION

Too many of us have allowed past failures to kill our passion. Remember the *real* people who received a good report from God in the "faith hall of fame." God entrusted His purposes to the hands of liars, murderers, whoremongers, deceivers, and cheaters.

Most of these people weren't "pretty," but they showed up when God asked for volunteers, and they got the job done despite their human imperfections. They put their trust in God, and He came through for them.

You can tell when God has touched people because they aren't arrogant. They aren't ashamed to tell people about their mistakes or where they came from. Their goal isn't to paint a pretty picture of their accomplishments; they just want to give glory to God and get the job done. They aren't afraid to roll up their sleeves and invade the ghettos, the highways, and the byways armed only with His love.

Where does the passion come from? How could they be so bold? They realize that if God hadn't touched them, they would have been dead anyway. They are thinking, *I'm living on borrowed time, and there's a charge to keep and a God to glorify.* Every day they see another sunrise, they tell themselves, "It is for *this cause* I have come—to bring others out of their pain and deliver them to the joy of my King and His kingdom."

To be honest with you, if I had let people deal with me, I wouldn't be here. I went through a divorce against my will, and all the church folk around me said, "God can't use you anymore. You're spoiled goods." But then I had a meeting with God. He said, "If you're willing to get up, then I have something for you. I never changed My mind about what I said over you the *first* time!"

Stop talking about what you did wrong. Start talking about what happened "right"! If you get on your knees, He will remind you about what He *put* in you. He will repeat what He has called you to do. I assure you that God has not changed His mind. Are you willing to change yours and line up with His Word?

Repent and turn from your sins and failures. Pick up that cross again and return to the first works! God will still use you. You can still obtain a good report along with all the other failures He transformed into heroes of heaven!

When you look at the roll call of saints in the book of Hebrews, remember that a divine passion flowed through each of them, no matter what they went through or how imperfect they were. And while that divine passion was driving them, God was fixing them up!

It's time to tell the truth and get right. What we really need to have is a little more truth in church instead of all that "testi-lying." We need to tell the truth about where we *really* came from and what we *really* did—and seal it with the truth about everything God really did. It's time to stop acting as if we are "without sin" and let the truth of God's love set someone else free!

· Chapter 12 ·

KINGDOM MEN, KINGDOM WOMEN

B oot camp is over; the certificate of completion is in your hand. Now you know what you believe. You know how to find the missing element of the kingdom. Perhaps you were once part of the problem, a man or woman "missing in action" with no plans to step back into the battle. It's too late to back out now. You know the truth, and it has set you free.

You're a *kingdom* person with the call of destiny beckoning you forward and upward. You know your life isn't your own because you've been bought with a price. That means there is no turning back. You are a person under authority because you know that in God's kingdom everyone is under submission. There is a chain of command here because we're not of the world. There must be a distinct difference between the two.

This overriding sense of the kingdom permeates everything we do and think about. Not one day goes by without our pondering the vast scope of God's design. This eternal kingdom reaches beyond the boundaries of time and space. It reaches all the way back to the beginning when God spoke the worlds into existence. It reaches forward beyond the point at which time will be no more, and it covers all points between.

We are learning as kingdom men and kingdom women joined together in marriage that the way we treat one another has a dramatic effect on the effectiveness of our prayers. If we refuse to settle a disagreement, then our family and God's kingdom purposes may suffer due to our lack of unity and agreement in prayer. This life really isn't about us—it is about Him and His purposes in the earth.

We've examined God's Word for guidance about His kingdom order for the home and marriage. Paul gave us the short version of an ancient answer:

> I want you to know that the head of every man is Christ, the head of woman is man, and the head of Christ is God . . . For a man indeed ought not to cover his head, since he is the image and glory of God; but woman is the glory of man. For man is not from woman, but woman from man. Nor was man created for the woman, but woman for the man. For this reason the woman ought to have a symbol of authority on her head, because of the angels. Nevertheless, neither is man independent of woman, nor woman independent of man, in the Lord. For as woman came from man, even so man also comes through woman; but all things are from God. (1 Cor. 11:3, 7–12)

We've discussed what a man wants (a kingdom woman who is uniquely equipped by God to operate in God's anointing) and what a woman needs (that rare commodity called a *kingdom man*). We've also asked why so many men are hiding from responsibility, and what God can do to cure the condition.

I'M STILL CONVINCED: MEN ARE RESPONSIBLE FOR EVERYTHING

In the final analysis, I'm still convinced that men are responsible for everything. A kingdom man is to "cultivate" his wife with the washing of the water of the Word. He is to gently mold her, shape her, and call her ministry and calling into being without compromising kingdom standards.

A kingdom man is called to stand, even if no one else (including his wife at rare times) is willing to stand with him. He is called and anointed to stand for the kingdom, speak into the lives of his family members, and tell them who they are and help them submit back and forth to one another. Above all, a kingdom man must know who he is and know the destiny God has for him, because the kingdom woman he married has come alongside to fulfill that destiny.

When we searched the Scriptures to see what God says about the virtues and strengths of women in the kingdom, we discovered that they have a particular anointing to be walking epistles and life givers to others.

I had the distinct privilege of talking for three hours with Coretta Scott King, the widow of Dr. Martin Luther King Jr. We met in her home, and I just talked with her and listened to this woman who was so full of grace and a deep knowledge of history.

Her grasp of details, facts, times, and places amazed me. I would call her the mother of a civil rights movement that not only blessed black people but also blessed the entire world.

In the midst of all of that, my mind was filled with questions I wanted to ask Mrs. King. I was trying to figure out how to handle the tension between my roles as a husband, a pastor, a father, and a leader in my community. How could I be a good husband to my wife while also answering the demands pulling on me from across the nation and the world?

Finally, I asked Mrs. King a simple question: "I know it is painful, and I know you had to give up a great deal and sacrifice a lot. But how did you deal with your husband and the call of destiny on his life?"

She looked at me with a broad grin and said, "First of all, it was fun. I really enjoyed it. When I married Martin, I did not just marry a man—*I married a destiny.* A lot of young women today do not understand that. But when God places a destiny on a man, you're not just marrying the man; you're marrying what God assigned to him."

As for the man, it is his responsibility to pursue God's purposes for his life with every ounce of passion he possesses. Dr. Ed Cole, author of *Maximized Manhood,* said something that really stuck with me. He said, "It is very hard for a woman to follow a 'parked car.'"

We also discovered the many pitfalls of "dating the devil" while searching for a saint to bring to the altar. The drama continued when we extended our audit of typical human behavior (as contrasted with kingdom standards) to the married side of the room.

The idea that "other people" might be populating the marriage bed sounded a bit controversial at first, but we discovered in God's Word that it was true! Fortunately, God's Word showed us how to do a housecleaning before bedtime rolled around again.

God Uses People in Spite of Their Weaknesses

We took things a step farther to examine the way God worked through some of the people described in the book of Hebrews, the people pulled aside for a date with destiny. The most amazing thing we learned was that these heroes of the faith were just average people who simply showed up when God called. He used them in spite of their personal weaknesses, fears, failures, sins, and odd quirks.

One of the things we must seek and preserve is the passion for life that God planted in each of us. We live in an environment dominated by "fire killers" who insist that everyone around them sink to the lowest common denominator of inspiration, zeal, holiness, courage, and service in the kingdom. God sees things differently. He delights in fanning the flames of our passion. He purifies us through the fires of adversity to help us bear even more fruit and affect even more lives than before.

The entire process of life in the kingdom boils down to our inner drive to know our God, to know one another, and on a more specific level, to love our spouses with a divine mix of purity and passion in the safety of the binding covenant commitment we call marriage.

Now It Is Up to You

What can we say in the end? Perhaps we should remind our-selves what James wrote toward the end of his earthly ministry. This apostle had imparted the things he received from Jesus; it was up to the people he had served to put into practice the things they had received from him. He wrote, "Therefore, to him who knows to do good and does not do it, to him it is sin" (James 4:17).

I recall the wisdom revealed in the ninth chapter of the book of Daniel, where Daniel said, "I, Daniel, understood *by the books* the number of the years specified by the word of the LORD through Jeremiah the prophet, that He would accomplish sev-enty years in the desolations of Jerusalem" (Dan. 9:2, emphasis mine). He was actually reading the writings and revelation God gave to another man named Jeremiah. Once Daniel received the revelation on that, he went into prayer with sackcloth and ashes and fasting.

I've said some things to you that are quite different. I've said some things that I suspect will arrest you and cause you to exam-ine who you are and who God called you to be.

If you really want to break through the old traditions in your heart and mind that God never placed there, then I ask that you follow in the footsteps of Daniel as you ponder the Bible truths in this book:

1. Go into prayer. Ask God to open your heart through His Spirit to the divine revelation behind my all-too-human words. It is the only way you will capture the living truth hidden behind my stammering human attempts to express them.

2. Follow the pattern of Daniel and repent in prayer for your sins. Do more than clear away the sins of your family. Confess and repent of the sins of your father and mother; repent of any sins committed by your grandparents and others in your bloodline. Extend your prayer of confession to cover the sins and shortcomings of your extended family members.

3. Pray a prayer of comparison. Begin to think about how good and faithful God is, compared with our unforgiving and unfaithful ways. Isaiah the prophet also followed this pattern the day he saw God "high and lifted up." He was in awe of the majestic sight before him in the temple, yet at the same time, he was painfully aware of his own sin. He cried, "Woe is me . . . I am a man of unclean lips" (Isa. 6:5). I am well aware of the value of the "in Christ" teachings about our true identity in God, but I am convinced that nothing can happen in the human soul until that person can honestly cry out to Him, "Woe is me, for I am undone!"

4. Finally, go into the prayer of commandment or spiritual declaration and entreaty. (This may only be done after we humble ourselves and repent of our sins. Otherwise it borders on the sin of presumption.) Daniel's prayer provides the best example and pattern for the prayer of declaration. He prayed, "O Lord, *hear!* O Lord, *forgive!* O Lord, *listen and act! Do not delay* for Your own sake, my God, for Your city and Your people are called by Your name" (Dan. 9:19, emphasis mine).

It was after Daniel prayed *this prayer* that Gabriel the archangel showed up with a message from God's throne (Dan. 9:20–27). After you pray, ask God to send ministering angels to minister to you, your spouse, your children, and all of those God has placed under your authority or spiritual covering. Once you reach this place, you will experience one of the greatest joys of the Christian life. You will possess the peace of God because His kingdom order has been restored. He is not the Author of confusion, but the Author of peace.

What have you received from this book? Do you know more about what you believe? Do you understand that *you* are part of the missing element in the earth? You know what a man—a kingdom man—wants, and you know what a kingdom woman needs. More important, you should have learned more about what the real King wants.

It Takes a Kingdom . . .

What will you do with what you know? What will you do with what you possess? The world is dying, and millions stand in the valley of decision. It will take more than a local church to save them. It will take more than a church denomination to break through with God's power and might. It will take a kingdom, an army of prayer warriors, prophets, preachers, evangelists, pastors, and teachers anointed to work together with no place for ego.

You know the truth about the kingdom now. Are you ready to join the battle and carry His glory and kingdom order into your workplace, onto the streets, into your neighbors' kitchens, and into the face of the adversary?

God isn't calling for churchgoers. He hasn't issued a summons for pew sitters. He's looking for someone with the anointing, with the passion to deliver the living flame of God to cold human hearts. He is calling forth a kingdom for such a time as this. Are you ready?

What does every man want? The woman God intends for him and a meaningful relationship with God. What does every woman need? A godly man who seeks the face of God in the evening and trusts Him for every good thing, and her own personal relationship with the heavenly Father.

NOTES

CHAPTER 1

1. From all of the comments I've heard from representatives from the female half of the human population, women seem to spend a good deal of time wondering and talking about what men really want (except for those hormonally charged moments when they are *sure* they know what a man wants).

2. James Strong, *Strong's Exhaustive Concordance of the Bible* (Peabody, MA: Hendrickson Publishers, n.d.), Greek, #2885, #2889.

3. This doesn't mean a woman should not stand up for what she believes or discuss important issues with authority and confidence. I'm saying that God gave man a sledgehammer for moving large resistant objects, and He gave woman a delicate but razor-sharp scalpel for delicate surgery that cannot be done with a hammer.

CHAPTER 2

1. I'm referring to Sarah's decision to give Abraham her Egyptian handmaiden, Hagar, as a wife or concubine so he could have a male successor (Gen. 16; 21; 25). Sarah didn't have the faith to believe God could cause her to become pregnant after so many years had passed. Abraham did have a son named Ishmael through Hagar, but this plan backfired when Sarah miraculously became pregnant and gave birth to Isaac. Ishmael was out and Isaac was in, but the enmity or bitter hatred between them would rage on through the centuries. It still rages today, and we felt the heat of its wrath when terrorists descended from Ishmael-guided commercial jetliners filled with innocent people into the World Trade Center Towers, the Pentagon, and a rocky field in Pennsylvania on September 11, 2001, as retribution for our friendship with Israel (the descendants of Abraham, Isaac, and Jacob).

2. Strong, *Strong's Exhaustive Concordance,* "double-minded" (Greek, #1374, from #1364 and #5590).

CHAPTER 3

1. Strong, *Strong's Exhaustive Concordance,* Greek, #5092, #5099.

2. Ibid., Greek, #1581, #1537, #2875.

CHAPTER 5

1. James Dobson, *Straight Talk to Men* (Nashville, TN: Thomas Nelson Publishers, 2000).
2. Ibid.
3. *Merriam-Webster's Collegiate Dictionary,* 10th ed. (Springfield, MA: Merriam-Webster, Inc., 1994), from the definition for *bar mitzvah,* 93.

CHAPTER 6

1. Strong, *Strong's Exhaustive Concordance,* Hebrew, #2332, # 2331.
2. Pastor Darlene Bishop's testimony was adapted from remarks she delivered to the New Birth congregation in partnership with my own remarks. The message was titled "Kingdom Men/Kingdom Women," tape #010-292, New Birth Missionary Baptist Church.

CHAPTER 7

1. Strong, *Strong's Exhaustive Concordance,* Greek, # 5413, #5414, #5342.

CHAPTER 8

1. Strong, *Strong's Exhaustive Concordance,* Hebrew, #3045. The past-tense form of *yada'* translated as "knew" appears ninety-eight times in ninety-eight verses. The present-tense form translated as "know" appears 964 times in 904 verses. By any measure, this is a universal term used to express an almost unlimited variety of ways to know, understand, perceive, share, join, become one, see, and become as something or someone. This is how James Strong defined *yada'*—"to know (prop. to ascertain by seeing); used in a great variety of senses, fig., lit., euphem. and infer. (including observation, care, recognition, and causat. instruction, designation, punishment, etc.) [as follow]:—acknowledge, acquaintance (-ted with), advise, answer, appoint, assuredly, be aware, [un-] awares, can [-not], certainly, for a certainty, comprehend, consider, X could they, cunning, declare, be diligent, (can, cause to) discern, discover, endued with, familiar friend, famous, feel, can have, be [ig-] norant, instruct, kinsfolk, kinsman, (cause to, let, make) know, (come to give, have, take) knowledge, have [knowledge], (be, make, make to be, make self) known, + be learned, + lie by man, mark, perceive, privy to, X prognosticator, regard, have respect, skilful, shew, can (man of) skill,

be sure, of a surety, teach, (can) tell, understand, have [understanding], X will be, wist, wit, wot."

CHAPTER 10

1. The writer of the book of Hebrews put it this way: "'My son, do not despise the chastening of the LORD, nor be discouraged when you are rebuked by Him; for whom the LORD loves He chastens, and scourges every son whom He receives.' If you endure chastening, God deals with you as with sons; for what son is there whom a father does not chasten? But if you are without chastening, of which all have become partakers, then you are illegitimate and not sons" (Heb. 12:5–8).
2. See Genesis 12:1–5.
3. See Genesis 12 for the remarkable events of Moses' first eighty years.
4. According to the Bible, Moses' authority was challenged by his older brother and older sister (Aaron and Miriam) on the pretext that he had done wrong by marrying an African woman. The Bible says, "Then Miriam and Aaron spoke against Moses *because of the Ethiopian woman whom he had married*" (Num. 12:1, emphasis added). God disagreed and personally defended Moses against the charges of his prejudiced family members (Num. 12:3–16).
5. Eddie Long, *Taking Over: Seizing Your City for God in the New Millennium* (Lake Mary, FL: Creation House, 1999), 100.

About the Author

When Bishop Eddie Long became the pastor of New Birth Missionary Baptist Church in Atlanta, Georgia, it had a membership of three thousand. Under his leadership, it has grown to approximately twenty-four thousand with members being added daily. As a result of his ministry practice of mentoring, 40 percent of his present church membership is men. He is currently the vice chair on the Morehouse School of Religion Board of Directors, is affiliated with the Traditional Values Coalition in Washington, D.C., and has served as area moderator of the American Baptist Churches of the South. Bishop Long has a daily radio program in Atlanta, Los Angeles, Miami, and London, England. Bishop Long and his wife, Vanessa, have four children.

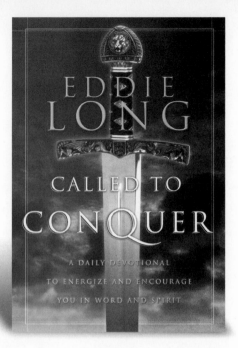

$\mathcal{I}$n this yearlong, 365-day format, each biblically based page contains a Scripture reading, a commentary, and a short prayer. The same robust and energetic style that makes Bishop Long a popular minister will also draw the reader into the pages of this book.

Long contends that many times a Christian can get excited about what God promises, but fails to take advantage of God's personal training programs. This day-by-day guide trains, comforts, and challenges.

ISBN 0-7852-6765-4

THOMAS NELSON
PUBLISHERS
Since 1798

www.thomasnelson.com